T0146857

MY AFFAIR WITH THE TRUNK MURDERESS

Kind of a Memoir

MELVIN MARKS

authorHOUSE®

AuthorHouse™
1663 Liberty Drive
Bloomington, IN 47403
www.authorhouse.com
Phone: 1 (800) 839-8640

Published by AuthorHouse   04/23/2015

ISBN: 978-1-5049-0919-8 (sc)
ISBN: 978-1-5049-0920-4 (e)

Library of Congress Control Number: 2015906404

Print information available on the last page.

Books by the same author

Jews among the Indians
Yesterday's Warriors

Anthologies

About Men: Reflections on the Male Experience
(Poseidon Press 1987)

To Bill, Tom, Pam, and of course to Mary

Acknowledgement

Big thank you to TMA PERITUS for their all around technical help, and much more.

I'm also indebted to Kurt Huber for his splendid cover design.

1

On A BLISTERING afternoon in 1937, my mother and I arrived at the railroad station on Jackson Street in Phoenix, Arizona. It was as hot as I can remember, an inferno. As we stepped off the train, grimy and spitting dust, we were hit with a blast of air that made even the stifling air of the train seem cool. We had spent four days and three nights in the coach car, munching on stale sandwiches or else making infrequent trips to the diner for meals my mother couldn't afford. It was a long, boring trip made to seem even longer because I had no inkling of exactly why we were going to Phoenix except that my mother had hay fever which had turned into asthma.

We had ridden the Rock Island all the way from Des Moines where I was born and had spent most of my life (all thirteen years to this point) and were heading for an unfamiliar place in the desert. I went along without protest, for I had little choice in the matter. And if I was able to protest I would scarcely have known how to form the words. I never even wondered why something like asthma was important enough to drive my mother and me from the home provided us by my great aunt and great uncle and their family, good people who took in homeless relatives like us. On the train, I remember the fear of being so far away from Des Moines and my friends, and of dreading the prospect of living in the unknown world that lay ahead.

The station platform was deserted when we arrived, and I recall having to drag our suitcases out of the depot in order to get a taxicab. My first glimpse of Phoenix wasn't the barren desert I had imagined.

The city was actually beautiful. There were palm trees everywhere, the buildings white or tan, scrubbed clean, reminding me of the scenes of Hollywood I'd seen one Saturday afternoon when my mother took me downtown to the Des Moines Theater to see Dick Powell and Rosemary Lane in _Hollywood Hotel_. Off to the north were the mountains, Camelback and Mummy by name, casting gigantic shadows over the desert. To me, fresh from the flat cornfields of Iowa, the landscape was so strange that it disconnected and frightened me. For a moment I wasn't sure of where I was. I held tight to my mother's arm, but I think she was as terrified as I was, for she was embarking on a journey into a strange land with no job, no friends and very little money.

I learned later that my mother had been trying to get out of Des Moines for a long time. She had visited Dr. Posner, the practitioner to Des Moines's Jewish community, about her asthma. Having no other answer to give her, he suggested she move to a warm, dry climate. He had planted a notion in her head that legitimized her escape from Des Moines and gave her a reason to say goodbye to our relatives. If there was any illness that was stress-related, hers was it, living as she had been, broke and unhappy, in a household not her own. There was never any speculation about the cause of her asthma because the concept of psychosomatic illness hadn't yet reached the provincial backwater that was Des Moines in those days; and even if it had, I doubt whether any of my relatives could have accepted such a notion. To them, God had simply handed her a fortune cookie and out had come a slip marked "asthma."

What was true about her then, and true up until the day she died in 1982, was her dependence on her brothers and sisters, her aunts and uncles, and on me, her only child. Even if she had been financially independent, she would still have been unable to leave the home of my aunt and uncle unless she had received permission from someone, anyone, even the iceman. With a benediction from someone else, no harm could possibly come to her. But permission from a doctor, a Jewish doctor at that, was like a signed affidavit from God. Now she could go to her relatives and borrow the money she needed to get a new start in a warm, dry climate.

I think I knew what she was up to. I couldn't put it together at the time, but as I think about it today, her ability to exaggerate her illness was the tip-off to what an accomplished actress she was. Later on I came to realize that her use of illness to gain sympathy, and to control her destiny, had become second nature. On me, her only child, she would orchestrate guilt trips that left me fearful and unhappy. If I had known what a guilt-ridden life lay ahead of me, I would have hit the road before the train got to Phoenix. I can say that today but, of course, I had no power then to make a break from my only parent, nor the courage to ask why I was being yanked out of school, nor the courage to question any of the major decisions that she made, or that others made for her, that were to deeply affect my own life.

My mother as well asked no questions but passively went along with even the worst of circumstances that came her way until such time as she could no longer endure them, and that is why we moved to Phoenix. Her inability to make decisions was not a lack of self-confidence but a deep emotional dependence, amplified I'm sure by her failed marriage. She had defied the advice of her family and married my father, a real sharpie. They were divorced in 1927, four years after they were married. So ended her defiance. No doubt the divorce was a humiliating experience, especially because marrying my father was the only time she took a stand against her family.

She had been warned that no good could come of it. My father, a traveling salesman, would come home from a week on the road with nothing to show for it, having spent his lonely evenings in lunatic poker games. He was one of the good old boys of the highway, everybody's pal, from Tulsa to Wichita, Kansas City to St. Louis. From his 1919 discharge from the army till his death in 1941, his life consisted of traveling––living from one day to the next in an endless sequence of dreary, third-rate hotels, the hobo jungles of the drummers where, invariably, there were white porcelain pitchers on the dressers along with flimsy hotel hand towels, the whole overly-sanitized place stinking of antiseptic.

My parents and I were living in Wichita at the time. One fateful Friday, my father came home after a week on the road, his pockets empty, the rent unpaid, his insurance having lapsed and no food in the house. My mother screamed that she was going home to Des Moines and taking me with her. While she packed, my father bent over my bed and sang "Sonny Boy" as he took his leave, the tears streaming down his cheeks. It was his last official act as a father. With age, the memory dims, so I can't guarantee the truth of certain events. This may have been one of them. I was three when I believe my father last sang to me, and I never saw him again. It is hard to imagine what a screwed-up time my parents had during their few years together, not to mention the even more screwed up life they bestowed upon me.

My curiosity about my father has never let up. What sort of man was he---bastard and bounder, or decent and loving? How was I to know? Just after my discharge from the army in 1945, I went to Wichita and talked with one of my father's friends, Henry Levitt, who my mother had mentioned to me several times. I remember feeling that I was doing an end-run around her, but so what? How long was I supposed to be kept in the dark? Henry ran a successful retail clothing business, and he was a solid citizen. He was the sponsor of a semi-pro basketball team called the Wichita Henrys. He had donated a lot of money to Wichita State University, and in return the school named its basketball stadium after him. Later on I would reflect with pride on how my old man, whom I never knew, became the good friend of the man who helped make Wichita State University a basketball powerhouse.

The feeling of pride it gave me in my father wasn't much, but it was all I had to go on. Mr. Levitt, by this time a very old man, still stood erect and wore clothes that were more elegant than was usual in Wichita. He had never seen me before but recalled that my father had a son, me, a kid named Arthur. But he spoke of my father as warmly as if they had been brothers. "I saw your father just a few days before he died," he said. "He came to the store and borrowed a dollar from me. He didn't have a dime to his name."

I hung on every word. He talked straight to me, without attempting to extol my father in any way. "Your father was a sick man," Henry said. "He gambled away every nickel he ever made." I had already heard those stories from my mother, who had been only too happy to tell them to me. But it fell to Henry Levitt to tell me more about him, news much more to my liking: that everybody loved Ben Randall (ne Rosenthal), that he was very smart and loved books, and that his winning ways with small town merchants made him, he said, "The best damn salesman who ever walked in my store." But it threw me when Henry referred to my father as being "sick." It was the first time I had heard that. To everyone else, he was simply a gambler, a vice-ridden no-goodnik who could have straightened himself out if he had chosen to. But by this time I knew better. He was a man who had no choices but one---a one-way ticket to moral and financial ruin. To put it in today's terms, his personal weapons of mass destruction were fifty-two playing cards and a game of five-card stud.

After I left Henry's store, I drove to Ottawa, Kansas, to visit the place where my father died. It happened in 1941 at an unmarked railroad crossing. He had made a sales call at Litwin's, a men's store on the main street of downtown Ottawa, and was driving to Kansas City when his car was struck by a train that ran only once a day between Lawrence and Kansas City. He was killed almost instantly. It was the second time I visited the site, and since then have returned a few more times. At the time of his death, there had been talk around Ottawa of the need to put up a gate at the crossing, but nothing had come of it.

What was curious about the site was that the railroad tracks ran parallel with the highway for several hundred yards before gradually crossing over the highway. I still wonder how my father could have driven alongside a train for so long without having been aware, gates or no gates, of its converging path toward the highway.

I have since concluded that the crash was not an accident. How could it have been? Imagine what his life must have been like. Dead broke, deeply in hock to his friends and the employers whose lines he carried, and probably lonely and dispirited as well. Maybe he even felt bad about never having paid a visit to his son, a question that will never be answered.

As I think about him driving alongside the train, I imagine what he might have been thinking---whether to step on the brakes and let the train pass or to hit the gas pedal and keep going. But unlike the kind of poker player he was, he chose, in a fleeting instant, to throw in the cards of his miserable life. I keep wondering what my own life would have been like if he had held his cards just a little longer. Would we have somehow wound up traveling the road together, I helping the old man carry his sample cases, pleading with him at his nighttime poker games, "C'mon, Pop, let's go, save some money for breakfast."

And as the years crept by, I would be there with him, wiping the nicotine-stained spittle from his lips, until it was time to douse his Blackstone cigar for the last time.

2

I N PHOENIX, MY mother and I checked into the San Carlos hotel downtown on Adams Street. Two days later she found a furnished apartment at 1508 North Central, Central then as now being the main north-south street. It didn't provide me with the privacy I longed for but did give me a more breathing room than I had in Des Moines. Best of all, it was our own, at least on paper. The matter of who was paying for it was temporarily forgotten. But once a month there arrived in the mail some stark reminders that my mother and I were still charity cases. Her brothers sent checks that ranged from 25 to 50 dollars. My mother tore open the envelopes, pulled out the checks and let the envelopes slide to the floor, scarcely glancing at the polite transmittal notes always written by her brothers' wives. That routine was so distasteful to me that I could never face her benefactors again without cringing. I vowed then that when I was able never to accept charity from a living soul.

The apartment had a kitchenette, a bath and a small, walk-in dressing room. There was a large living room with a small balcony that looked west on McDowell Road. My mother slept on a studio couch and I on an in-a-door bed. The building's apartments, six in all, were on the second floor of a two-story masonry building with a fake adobe exterior. The ground floor was occupied by retail stores.

The building hasn't changed much. Actually it's better looking now, having had many facelifts over the years. As I pass it today on my visits to Phoenix, the old memories seem to protrude through the walls. I think about all the people I knew, easily recalling their faces but straining to come up with their names. But not so with Myrna Handmacher, Floyd Antonelli and Katherine Antonelli. And, yes, Ruth Judd---you may know her as Winnie Ruth---the seductive blond butcher. I think of them still. They are never out of my mind even though many years have gone by since I last saw them. They are so far removed from my earlier years in Des Moines that it seems as if I've lived two different lives, separate and distinct except for the impact one set of memories has had on the other. Those years in the desert were a bittersweet mixture--- years of torment, years of bliss. Even though I would never want to live through them again, I still think about them. I can't let go.

I still visit Phoenix three or four times a year. Ask me what I do there? The answer is: not much. Mostly I cruise around, trying to dredge up old memories, astonished that the city, now the sixth largest in the nation, is so different today from what it was in 1937 when I stood in front of the Westward Ho Hotel and heard the loudspeaker announce that Doug Corrigan had flown the wrong way across the Atlantic. Then I drive by the Arizona State Hospital at Twenty-fourth and Van Buren where Winnie Ruth Judd spent so much of her life. The old grey stone building, from which she had escaped so often, has been demolished and replaced with one-story dormitories.

My route next takes me west on Van Buren Street along a wretched corridor of cheap motels and bars---hookers on every corner---and then finally past Phoenix Union High, my old high school, long since closed.

From there I turn north on Central Avenue, along the way straining to remember where Gross's delicatessen was located. I continue up Central to McDowell Road, to our old apartment building where, down the corridor from us, Floyd Antonelli lived with his mother, Katherine. As I wheel my car around the torturous curves of my past life, I think I can still hear the sounds of "Besame Mucho" floating out of the juke box at Grosso's Drive-In, which was located next door to our apartment building.

Besame, besame, mucho
Each time I bring you a kiss
I hear music divine
Besame, besame mucho

The song swirls around in my brain while I drive the same route, over and over, never tiring of it. The old sights are gone, blown away by time, but the ghosts are still there, only for me: Arthur Randall, boy dreamer, forever at one with the past.

THE YEAR WE arrived in Phoenix, Joe Louis knocked out Jimmy Braddock at Madison Square Garden and won the heavyweight championship of the world. Not that the date is so important to me; it's just that I was an only child, and we only children remember everything. We suck up information like a Dustbuster. There are no siblings to divert us or compete with us, so as an antidote to loneliness we hound dictionaries and reference books and daydream our way through life. I have won the doubles title at Wimbledon playing alongside George Lott. I've tap danced the socks off of Bill Robinson as the only ofay act at the Regal Theatre in Harlem. There was no end to what I could do during those Phoenix years, alone and unnoticed.

Phoenix in 1937 was a desert community of 60,000 sun-parched souls. Many were Mexicans and Indians, along with a sprinkling of blacks and Chinese in numbers small enough to go almost unnoticed. The Mexicans and non-whites lived in shacks around Buckeye Road, the southernmost boundary of the city proper. Occasionally I would wander down there, standing around, surveying the scene, my mission unclear, except that I was horny at the sight of Mexican women seated in the darkened bars. I identified with Buckeye Road and its people. I was comfortable around them. It was a broad street lined on both sides with flophouses, pawn shops, cantinas and cheap cafes. The sun beat down mercilessly all over town but nowhere, it seemed, with such fury as on Buckeye Road where the Mexican men wearing Levis, western boots and ten-gallon straw hats slouched in doorways or, weaving from too much *cerveza*, argued on the sidewalks with slatternly Mexican women. The women had large sloping breasts and wore skirts too tight around their asses. The sight of them was an enticing spectacle to a boy my age.

From Buckeye Road, the city extended north through the downtown district, past the main east-west streets of Van Buren, Pierce, Taylor and Roosevelt, and continued a few more blocks to McDowell, the northern edge of the central city. Phoenix was later to expand rapidly to the north, an expansion that was just becoming evident with newer homes located beyond McDowell at Encanto Park, a spacious, well-kept city park, Here stood elegant two-story Spanish style residences, set back off quiet, palm-lined streets, the showplaces of physicians, lawyers, automobile dealers, bankers and wealthy Jewish merchants. These were the native Arizonans, the early arrivals and their offspring. Although they did not post "no trespassing" signs, they were nevertheless there in my mind, glowing like neon whenever I approached the neighborhood. It had been the same way in Des Moines when I ventured onto the west side of town where the affluent lived. Temple B'nai Jesherum, a reform congregation, their stronghold, where the German Jews, along with those who wished they were, didn't wear yarmulkes. They were presided over by Eugene Manheimer, an aristocratic rabbi. There, no Jews stood on the sidewalk after Services, gesturing, schmoozing and discussing the World Series, as they did in front of Tifereth Israel, the conservative synagogue where my bar mitzvah was held. Instead, these were *drei tag Juden*, three day Jews making a fast retreat, for fear of being seen by the gentiles because they didn't want to appear to be holding ad hoc sidewalk conclaves, as the Jews from Tifereth Israel did.

That first year in Phoenix, I had no friends. I enrolled in the eighth grade at Kenilworth School and rarely got a second glance from my classmates. If anything, they went out of their way to make me feel unwelcome. They were an inbred group, wary of outsiders, especially the lungres, those who came to Phoenix for pulmonary reasons and were not sons and daughters of the pioneers.

"We have a new student with us," said the teacher, addressing the class that first day. "Stand up and tell the class your name. Up, up, nice and tall." Her name was Alicia Baldwin, and she was a tall woman with very short brown hair and an abrupt manner.

I rose slowly from my seat. "Arthur R-r-randall," I stammered.

There were snickers.

"Now tell the class where you come from, Ar-THUR," she said, coming down hard on the second syllable.

"Des Moines, Iowa," I said obediently, my legs trembling. My reply brought some snickers.

"Des Moines, hmm? I've not had the pleasure," she said. "Have any of you, students?"

No hands were raised.

I remember wishing that she'd drop dead on the spot.

"Where did you attend school in Des Moines?" she asked. "I'm sure the class would like to know."

"Washington Irving Junior High." I was careful not to volunteer any information she didn't ask for.

"I see." She looked away from me, and then said to the class. "Do any of you know who Washington Irving was?"

There were no replies.

'Well, perhaps you can enlighten the class, Ar-THUR, or don't you know either?"

"Yes, mam, I know."

"Then will you be kind enough to tell us, please?"

"He wrote a book," I said. She would have to pry the answer out of me.

"And that book was..."

The Legend of Sleepy Hollow, I said, reluctantly.

"Very good. You can sit down now."

And then, just to make sure she didn't have the last word, I added another book. Tales of the Alhambra.

She coughed in embarrassment.

I looked around the room. The snickering was still going on. It was clear that I would never make friends in this school. I didn't dress like the others. I wore the clothes my father had sent me, the latest in boys' apparel from one of the lines he sold. Boys my age in Phoenix wore dirty Levis with their shirttails hanging out. I still have a picture of my eighth grade graduating class at Kenilworth. There were perhaps one hundred students in the photograph, and as I look at it today---at the grimy faces and filthy Levis and the girls in dresses below their knees---I can't pick out a single classmate I remember. After my first day, I pleaded with my mother to buy me a pair of Levis. Mistakenly, I thought that being properly attired (or improperly, as the case may have been) would improve my social life. But no such luck. I was not one of them, and never would be.

I TURNED FOURTEEN that summer and got a job delivering the *Arizona Republic*, the morning newspaper. My mother had already found work at the regional office of the U.S. Treasury Department, Bureau of Public Debt. It was a Civil Service clerical job, grade 1 or grade 2, I forget which. But more important, I fell in love with a woman down the hall from our apartment, a buxom blonde waitress who worked the swing shift at a restaurant downtown.

Her name was Katherine Antonelli. I rarely saw her wearing anything but a housecoat over her nightgown, her mammoth breasts never fully concealed. Before my mother found a job, Katherine would come to our apartment and the two of them would drink coffee. I sat around and listened to them talk and stared sidelong at Katherine's breasts until she became aware of what I was doing. Then she would tug self-consciously at the top of her housecoat, pulling it close around her neck, and with that it was my turn to leave the apartment and go for a ride on the second-hand bike my mother bought me. No bike, no paper route.

I wasn't happy about having a second-hand bike after once owning a brand-new, bright-red J.C. Higgins in Des Moines. The bike had been a birthday gift from my father. It arrived on a Sears Roebuck truck. Although my mother sneered when she saw it, it provided me with the happiest few months of my life. But a few weeks before my bar mitzvah, the same Sears truck came back and picked up the bike. It hadn't been paid for, the driver said. My mother sneered again. I don't remember making a fuss. My great aunt said that it was God's will. Hardly that. By this time I knew that my father was a deadbeat and the good Lord had nothing to do with it. Still, I never could muster any feelings of hatred toward my father.

ALL THAT SUMMER, I delivered papers at dawn, and for the rest of the day thought about Katherine. A few times I saw her in the hallway late at night, entering her apartment with a stranger. As I had it figured, it was some guy she had picked up at the restaurant. I would imagine her in bed, unsnapping her brassiere and unleashing those big breasts, which would fall to each side in gigantic heaps. It was a scene I couldn't erase from my mind, and I kept thinking about it until I almost went crazy.

Katherine had a son about two years older than me. Most of the time he lived with his father in Salt Lake City, but occasionally returned for indefinite periods to stay with his mother. When we first met I was fifteen and had just finished my freshman year at Phoenix Union High. We would pass each other in the corridor of the apartment building without speaking. He stopped me one day as I was entering our apartment.

"You must be Artie Randall," he said, holding out his hand. "I'm Floyd Antonelli. My mother told me about you."

"Yeah, I'm Arthur," I said, croaking in embarrassment. "Glad to meet you." I was sure he knew about my having sex with his mother, even if I was only imagining it. Things like that have a way of being leaked.

Floyd and I saw a lot of each other during the next several weeks. I liked him. He knew the score. He got the joke. Might I even say he had the mind of a bona fide degenerate Floyd was up front with it, and though I was inclined the same way, I channeled such thoughts into the dark alleys of Guilt City.

Even though he had been kicked out of PUHS, he hung around the school a lot, trying to make out with the girls. He was a master at that. I watched him operate, awestruck by his technique. He was casual, witty, and so full of baloney it made my head swim. Floyd made no distinctions; all girls were prospects, black, white or Hispanic. But not the Indian girls. They attended their own school out on Indian School Road. He'd have hung around there, too, except there was no way he could pass as a student.

I heard him call out to me one afternoon as I was walking down the center corridor of the main building of the high school.

"Hey, Artie, Artie, wait up."

Through the years, PUHS---as the school was known---had served nearly all the high school kids in Phoenix, including both Barry Goldwater and his younger brother, Bob; Steve Allen; Bill Mauldin; and several Arizona governors. Its enrollment was well over 4,000. The school fronted both Van Buren Street and Seventh Street. With its three multi-story buildings and Montgomery Field, the new football stadium, PUHS looked more like a college campus than a high school.

I tried hard to downgrade my attire in high school. I had always been aware of my appearance. Every now and then, when I lived in Des Moines, my father would send me the latest in boys' clothing, samples from one of his lines. Annabel Knobloch, a domestic who worked for my aunt, used to wash and iron them to perfection, with me watching her every move. I hadn't changed a bit since those years in Des Moines. Only now perfection was the last thing I wanted. I was dressing like the rest of the Phoenix kids. I took to wearing my shirt-tail outside my Levis, the Levis themselves filthy. But no matter, I was still not one of them. I was an outsider, the son of a transplanted "lunger" from the East, and a Jew to boot. I had grown a bit but was still small for my age. My face had become dark from the sun, as dark as a Mexican's, and a smudge of facial hair had appeared on my upper lip, not enough to warrant shaving, though. There was plenty of time for that, my mother said, just after she mentioned how messy I looked.

Floyd drew up alongside me. "Hey, Artie, pullyercocktoday?"

"Whadja say, Floyd?"

"Pullyercocktoday, Artie." He paused to let the words sink in.

"Whadja say?"

I said, "It's pretty hot today."

"Yeah, I heard ya, you moron."

Floyd was a tall, heavy-set boy, fair-skinned and red cheeked. His blond hair was worn long and combed straight back without a part. I couldn't figure out why his face was usually damp with perspiration, as much during the winter months as during the intense heat of summer. I also didn't understand why someone with a name like Antonelli looked the way Floyd did. In the movies, guys with names like that looked like George E. Stone in *Little Caesar* or like Marc Lawrence in *San Quentin*—swarthy guys who sneered and talked out of the sides of their mouths. They certainly didn't look the way Floyd did, like Nelson Eddy in *Naughty Marietta*.

"Artie, old pal, I want to ask you something."

"Sure."

"Will you be straight with me?"

"You know me," I said, "I'm the original Ralston Straight-shooter. So what do you want?"

"What I want to know, Artie, is … d'ya eat shit?"

"What?"

"I said, did ya eat yet?"

Floyd roared with laughter at his own joke then bent into a boxer's crouch and began sparring with me in the hallway, throwing jabs with his left and flicking his nose with his right thumb.

"Cut it out, Floyd. I go to school here. Do you want to get me kicked out? What are you doing here, anyway?"

"Katherine said I have to get educated, so I'm getting educated." He began singing the PUHS fight song. *"Phoenix Coyotes/Oh Phoenix Coyotes/Phoenix Coyotes we're all for you…"*

"Okay, I'll bite. Who is she?"

"Why should I tell you?"

"C'mon, Floyd, maybe I know her. Maybe she sits in front of me and I dip her pigtails in my inkwell."

"In the first place she's a senior and she wouldn't be in any of your classes, and in the second place she's too smart to sit that close to a turd like you."

"Are you going to tell me who she is or not?"

"Why is it so important?"

"Because I'm Philip Marlowe, my client needs the information."

"You're crazy, Artie, you see too many movies and you jerk off too much."

"Twice last night, is all."

"Yeah, I'll bet. And even if you did you'll never pass the old master," Floyd said. "Broke my all-time record the other day---three times in an hour and a half, right in the crapper of the Orpheum theater. I got so horny I had to walk out of the theater three times."

"What show did you see?"

"Draegerman's Courage."

"Hmm, what's it about?"

"Great movie. These guys get caught in a mine cave-in and Barton Maclaine burrows into the ground and saves them."

"You got a boner watching Barton Maclaine burrowing into the ground? Jesus."

"Hell, yes," Floyd said, "wouldn't you?"

"Everything gives me a boner," I said. "Who was the girl?"

"Jean Muir."

"I don't think she's too sexy."

"I wouldn't kick her out of bed," Floyd said.

We walked out of the front door of the school. "Where you going, Artie?"

"Home," I said. "I gotta get the house cleaned up before my mother comes back."

"Where is she?"

"Went to LA. She'll be back later tonight."

"What did she go there for? Is she taking a screen test? Jesus, Artie, maybe she'll be a movie star and I can jerk off at her first movie."

"Beautiful. That's really beautiful, Floyd."

"Just kidding."

3

WE LEFT THE school and walked north on Seventh Street. I had learned quite a bit about Floyd in the weeks I had known him. As he related the story to me, Katherine divorced Floyd's father in Cleveland in 1934. Mother and son then left Cleveland, Katherine settling in Phoenix while Floyd's father, who worked for the Erie Lackawana, found a job with the Union Pacific in Salt Lake City. Four years later, his father married a Mormon woman with two children, both of whom were considerably younger than Floyd. Theirs was an agreeable union, according to Floyd, and although his stepmother wasn't unkind to him, Floyd felt like an intruder in his father's home. His stepmother's children received most of the attention, and it seemed to Floyd that his father had written him off and wasn't concerned any longer about his future.

Floyd got kicked out of school in Salt Lake, just as he had in Phoenix. The principal of his high school, a strict Mormon, told Floyd's father that even though Floyd was likeable enough, he was lazy and unable to apply himself and, what's more, his personal conduct was as poor as his grades. He'd been fooling around with a couple of Mormon girls, and that was the real reason he was kicked out, Floyd told me, not the bad grades.

I remembered thinking that I'd gladly have given up school if I could have done it with some Mormon gals. Floyd said they were hot as hell. But as I think about it, these same girls would finally settle down and marry guys whose hair was combed over their ears and who wore polyester suits and looked like the singers on the Lawrence Welk show.

I couldn't resist thinking about Katherine as Floyd talked about the Latter Day Saints gals. Maybe she was as horny in her way as Floyd was in his. Like mother, like son. But the thought of being in the sack with her was too frightening to consider. Not with my best friend's mother. Jesus, no.

Floyd told me he wasn't any happier living with his mother than with his father. But he had more freedom with Katherine because she was away from the apartment so much of the time, either working or dating some of the men she'd met at the hotel. Meanwhile, Floyd picked up spending money doing odd jobs, shuttling between parents whenever he felt the urge. Occasionally, Katherine or his father gave him money, and his father, through his railroad connections, paid Floyd's fare between Phoenix and Salt Lake.

FLOYD AND I had two things in common. We both lived with our mothers, he part-time, I full-time, and we were children of divorce. I have to say that my own life was far more complicated than his. My mother and I had always lived in the home of relatives, continually fearful of being tossed out on the street if we created problems for them. No two ways about it: we were charity cases who had to be on our best behavior.

My mother was part of a family of money lenders who had arrived in Iowa from Lithuania late in the nineteenth century. My grandmother, Dora, was the sister of the family's patriarch, old Jake Levich; Old Jake had three other siblings. One was my great Aunt Ida with whom we lived; another was Abe Levich who also lived in the household. Most profited from their relationship with Old Jake; he had gotten their husbands, nephews and sons-in-law started in the loan business. Their children and their children's children also profited from Old Jake's brand of feudalism.

But not my grandmother. Dora and my grandfather, Joe, who went their own way, for whatever reason, and thus they became the poor relatives. I was still very young when the Levich dynasty was being built, but I might have been included later on, God help me, if I hadn't been the grandson of Dora and Joe and if my mother's marriage hadn't failed and if---big if---I hadn't been puny and shy and of no importance to anyone, even to myself.

I saw Jake on Sunday afternoons when he came to Aunt Ida's for lunch, our main meal. When he arrived, we took our seats at the dinner table and began eating. Jake sat at the head of the table in my Uncle Louis's chair, and I've long wondered how Uncle Louis felt about giving up his regular seat. But as I later found out, Jake had set up Uncle Louis in the loan business. And that explained that. I remember thinking that I would never give up my seat at the head of the table in my own home, no matter to whom, job or no job.

Jake was short and stocky, with steel gray hair and a clipped moustache, and he spoke with a pronounced accent. I hated the sonofabitch, although I didn't have the courage even to think it, much less to say it. I was also terrified of him. I'm told that he detested his wife and rarely brought her to Sunday dinner. He rarely spoke to me but grudgingly accepted me for what I was, a negligible little *pisher* in my aunt's home.

Once, as the time to begin studying for my bar mitzvah was approaching, he beckoned me to his side at the head of the dinner table. All eyes were on me. "Ar-tur," he said, so that all could hear, "if you study hard and become bar mitzvah, I'll make sure to pay for your college education."

There were approving nods around the table. My mother whispered that I should thank Old Jake. On cue, I said, "Gee, thanks a lot, Uncle

Jake," getting as much feeling into the words as I could, trying to make it sound like he'd just rescued me from drowning.

He made a few grunting sounds of acknowledgement, and with that, my aunt brought him his customary shot glass of schnapps. That marked the conclusion of dinner. Then, as usual, we all got up, and Jake headed for the living room couch for a nap.

I have to admit that whatever homage was paid to the old boy was well-deserved. He and his family had come from the old country and wound up in Des Moines after a stop on the eastern seaboard. He had begun as a peddler in Iowa, but that was short-lived. His sights were set higher. He started in the consumer finance business from the ground up, that ground being a spot in front of Davidson's Furniture store on Fifth and Walnut. There he passed out cards advertising loans of two dollars, in return for a three-dollar payback. There were no usury laws in Iowa at the time, and those fortunate enough to have an office were able, under a cloak of reputability, to charge, with few squawks, a minimum of 36 percent interest per annum on the unpaid balance, sometimes more. Old Jake's business was successful from the beginning and eventually grew into a successful national company.

My mother, whose dependency continued to deepen, eventually was referred to, behind her back, as "Poor Arlene," and I, her son, as "Poor Arthur." Never directly in front of us, but often within earshot. Neither of us shook free of the reference until we arrived in Phoenix. But by that time, my mother had made a career of living up to being "poor Arlene," while I in turn tried to keep from retching when that "poor Arthur" reference was applied to me. Jake, in due course, welshed on his promise of sending me to college. Just as well. World War II and the G.I. Bill got him off the hook.

I RETURNED TO Des Moines during the summer of 1940 ostensibly to escape the unmerciful heat of Phoenix only to find myself working for a man named Hans, an export from Germany who had recently arrived in Des Moines. He had been working as a stock clerk at Younker Brothers, the city's foremost department store, when he married Beatrice's eldest daughter. Either as a wedding gift or a bribe, Beatrice bought them a dry goods store in Nevada, Iowa, a small farm community with one main street and only oblivion on either side. Beatrice figured that since Hans's family had owned a store of the same type in Munich, he would find the store in Nevada (which carried work boots, denim and Sunday-go-to-meeting clothes) enticing.

She was wrong. Nevada was not Des Moines or Munich, and my time there was limited to two days, one day less than the new owners. Hans, who my cousin Moose dubbed "Han-sie the Nazi," then became vice-president of Beatrice and her husband's loan company. And that was the last I saw of the money-lenders, and of Nevada, Iowa.

That summer of 1940, Moose and I resorted to a life of petty thievery, targeting my grandmother Dora, who lived in a rooming house on Des Moines's east side. Dora, Jake Levich's sister, was balmy, but balmy in nice way, allowing her great nephews to steal money from the top of her dresser, only nickels and dimes, but still a generous act on her part, like leaving milk and cookies for Santa Claus. She had suffered from intestinal problems and found a measure of relief from a potent prescription, so it came as no surprise when, either because she was high on paregoric or else overcome by the demons that rattled around in her head, she walked into the Racoon River one day and drowned.

I had wondered why my mother moved into Aunt Ida's home after she left my father, but I soon concluded that her aunt was a far more suitable parent for her than her own mother.

In her aunt my mother found a perfect surrogate mother, a woman who was loving, generous and very kind to her, often at the expense of her own five children. I remember her as a short, stocky woman with gnarled hands. She wore her hair short and spent most of her days in the kitchen, where she did all of the cooking for the household. Huge platters of beef, kishka and potatoes were standard evening fare, the beef having first been soaked in buckets of salt water to remove the blood.

My Uncle Louis, having freed himself from Old Jake's clutches, did something involving cattle, exactly what I can't say, but he left the house early in the morning wearing rubber boots and returned in the afternoon, his boots covered with mud and cow shit. Curious as I was, I never asked about the cow shit. In those days and in that household, you didn't ask questions. You kept your mouth shut and wrote your own version of the news.

MY AUNT'S HOUSE was very small. My mother and I shared a tiny bedroom with room for only one bed, and so I had to sleep in the same bed with her until I was nine. After that, a small corner of the attic became my sleeping quarters. There was only one bathroom, and if it was occupied when I needed to use it, I had to be on the alert and ready to jump when I heard the toilet flush.

Twelve of us lived in the house. In addition to my great aunt and uncle and their five children, there was my mother and me; my great grandmother Rachel; my great uncle Abe; and Annabel, the live-in servant girl who did the cleaning, washing and ironing in return for board and room and a few dollars a week.

A stubby young woman with a lantern jaw who wore her blonde hair in tight little curls, she had recently been released from the girls' reformatory at Mitchellville, Iowa. She, too, slept in the attic. Often, I recall, she would go to the Tromar Ballroom where the big dance bands played one-night stands. One time she returned with a big crush on Ted Fio Rita, a good-looking orchestra leader. Sometime after that, Moose and I discovered under her bed a dildo standing upright in an empty can of MJB coffee. The discovery left me scratching my head for the next several weeks. What was that imponderable thing and what did Annabel do with it? I was just beginning to feel the distracting, non-specific yearnings of puberty, so I asked Moose to explain what dildos were for. After that, I paid frequent visits to Annabel's coffee can---which, by this time, had become a sort of shrine---and stared at the dildo without ever touching it.

God forbid.

MY GREAT UNCLE Abe was a veteran of the Spanish-American War and a bachelor. He spent most of the day sitting in his small room playing Solitaire and seldom left it except to visit the barber shop at Thirteenth and Forest. He was a short, crotchety man who had spent most of the war in an army hospital, suffering from dysentery.

One morning when I was twelve, I went to his room to awaken him for breakfast. I remember noticing his pallor and the frozen look on his face. Something was wrong. I shook him a few times and shouted, "Uncle Abe, Uncle Abe!" But he didn't respond. I ran downstairs to get Aunt Ida. I heard myself screaming, "Come quick! Something's wrong with Uncle Abe!"

He had died during the night of a heart attack. I remember being unmoved by his death, for he was not an endearing man. With his death, however, came my release from the attic, and I immediately moved into his room. It had a single, dim light overhead, which marked the beginning of my interest in reading. I read a lot---books like *Seventeen, The Prince and the Pauper*, and *The Last of the Mohicans*. There were also the eight-pagers that Moose gave me. These booklets depicted comic strip characters having sex---Maggie and Jiggs, Blondie and Dagwood, Harold Teen and others banging their brains out.

Whenever I think about Uncle Abe, it is usually with strong feelings of guilt. I should have been unhappy that he died, but I didn't feel a thing, not a ripple of regret. And then there was the matter of my gross breach of respect, for there should have been an interval of mourning between his death and my reading those eight-pagers right there on the very bed where he used to sleep. I seldom think about Uncle Abe, Aunt Ida, old Jake and the others; they have all passed on, of course. But the imprint of my having been a well-behaved charity case still is evident even now, in my old age.

AS A CHILD in Des Moines I was unaware that there was any life other than that of an Orthodox Jew. In my house, Yiddish and English were spoken interchangeably, and the Jewish dietary laws were scrupulously observed. I could never understand why dishes and silverware used for meat had to be kept separate from silverware and dishes used for dairy. No one ever offered me an explanation, and I never asked for one. Like all other aspects of my life, I went along, being the obedient resident orphan. Somewhere in the back of my mind, I'm sure, was the feeling that if I violated the Jewish dietary laws I would not only be banished from my aunt's home but would be sent to a place in Hell reserved especially for rebellious kids who washed down their pot roast with a glass of milk.

While I was studying for my bar mitzvah, a Jewish family from Winnipeg, Canada, moved to Des Moines. They were friends of my aunt and my mother. The father, Alec Walters, made dentures for a living and (as I overheard) fooled around with *shiksas*; his wife, Evelyn, with whom he was continually in dispute, was a cheerful redhead whom I deduced was a little wild herself. Their son, Beryl, and I became friends, and we remained friends until my mother and I moved to Phoenix.

In what was to be a watershed experience for me, Evelyn took Beryl and me to a restaurant called Canfield's, out on Fleuer Drive near the Des Moines Water Works, for barbecue ribs. It was the most memorable meal I have ever eaten. The ribs were succulent, crisp and absolutely delicious. That evening marked my fall from Grace, and I've spent the rest of my life not seeking redemption but searching (mostly in vain) for ribs that tasted that good.

I DON'T BELIEVE that Aunt Ida and Uncle Louis were nearly as strict about attending *shul* as they were about observing the Jewish rituals---such matters as spitting upon hearing bad news in order to ward off evil spirits, or covering the mirrors in their home upon returning from a funeral. It wasn't until I was older that I learned that Uncle Louis, in yet another ritual, had taken my mother to Kansas City for a "*Get,*" a Jewish divorce, as if her civil divorce was not sufficiently binding in the Good Lord's eyes.

One unpleasant landmark of my childhood was my mandatory attendance at Hebrew School where I prepared for my bar mitzvah. As it turned out, I was a big success, my first genuine triumph. The only sour note was the rabbi's bad breath. An old lady gave me a present of the *Old Testament*. She inscribed it: *"Arthur, dear, yours was the most beautiful bar mitzvah I ever heard."* I showed her gift to my cousin Moose, and he told me he had received the same gift from the same lady with the identical inscription. I pointed out that because the inscription came a year after his, it therefore superseded his, a view he refused to accept. Moose was a very good athlete who was a year older than me and could do most things better, among them having been a high-scoring forward on the University of Iowa basketball team and a ranked tennis player in the Midwest.

It was too bad I was snatched away from Des Moines on the heels of my only moment of triumph. But as usual, my mother's illness came first.

4

BACK IN PHOENIX, I continued to be obsessed with Katherine. She was ever-present in my thoughts---a pretty woman but thick-set, like Floyd. She lashed her big breasts tightly to her body in the fashion of the time, and was happy and touchingly feminine. Rarely on her days off from the restaurant would she venture into the sun, preferring instead to lounge around her apartment in her housecoat, smoking and sipping wine. Her long blond hair blended with her pale complexion.

She liked visiting with Arlene, and I looked for her each time I opened the door to our apartment. The hope of seeing her there was the big reason I had for going home. Just the sight of her housecoat falling open, giving me a glimpse of the white flesh of her thigh, started me panting, and I would nearly faint. Often, she threw me a quick smile and looked at me as if she knew what I was thinking. And the times I encountered her in the hallway she would lightly brush up against me, and a faint smile would cross her lips.

But then I would start thinking about old Jake, imagining he was monitoring all my thoughts and giving me the hard stare and wagging his stubby fingers at me. And Uncle Abe, who was just as reproachful, shaking a card at me---a one-eyed Jack from his Solitaire game---and making a jerk-off motion with his other hand. They had my number, those two---two punishing gods who would never grant me a reprieve, not until the day I died.

SHORTLY AFTER I met him, Floyd got into trouble. He told me the entire story, and I never asked questions about it or brought up the matter again. He had been arrested for stealing a shirt and tie from Goldwater's Department Store, but because he had never been in trouble before, the Juvenile Court judge let him off with only a scolding and a warning. His arrest was the turning point in the relationship with his parents, and from then on, it seemed, they gave up on him and became less interested in his welfare.

He never told either of his parents that the shirt and tie wasn't for himself but was intended as a birthday gift for his father. But that's the kind of guy Floyd was.

ONE TIME, MY mother gave us money for dinner at Grosso's. We ordered hamburgers and cokes. While the waitress was serving us she spilled most of my coke on the counter, but gave no indication that she was going to refill my glass. Then Floyd raised all kinds of hell about it and said he'd never come back to this crummy joint again. I tried to keep him quiet because I liked Grosso's. It had the best juke box in town, Claude Thornhill's rendition of "Polka Dots and Moonbeams" and Benny Carter playing "Melancholy Lullaby." Floyd always fought for his rights; actually, mine more than his own.

AFTER SCHOOL ONE day, Floyd and I walked west on Roosevelt Street in silence, heading toward Central. It was October, but still blazing hot. Only a few pedestrians were on the street: some men in short-sleeve shirts, open at the collar, a group of high school boys in red and black Coyote t-shirts, and an old lady carrying a fringed umbrella. Even in October, few people were courageous enough to venture outside, and the city was desolate. Work shifts commenced early, as they did in mid-summer, and ended in the middle of the afternoon.

Then, suddenly, Floyd dropped a bomb. He made a statement that was to change my life. He told me that Winnie Ruth Judd had escaped. It didn't mean much to me at the time. Even though I was delivering the *Arizona Republic* every morning, I only read the sports section.

"Who's Winnie Ruth Judd?" I remember asking him.

"Oh, nobody special," Floyd said, "just some broad who shot her two roommates, then carved up their bodies and stuffed them in a railroad express trunk. That's all."

"So? What about her?"

"She escaped last night. She was in the crazy house, over on Van Buren."

"You mean here? Here on Twenty-fourth Street?"

"Yeah, I mean here, just a few blocks from your paper route."

I began to shiver. "You're kidding me, aren't you?"

"I wish I were," he said. "When she gets hold of a knife, watch out. She goes straight for your johnson."

"Jesus."

"Artie, I'll tell you the truth---her being on the loose scares the be-Jesus out of me. Everybody in Phoenix is scared. My mother doesn't want to come home alone at night after work. The cops think Winnie Ruth's right here in town. The paper says she's got no dough to travel, No hideout either. No one wants to touch her. There's some kind of politics involved. The story's in today's paper. If you knew how to read, Artie, you'd have the sheet on her. Anyway, I'm going to Utah for a couple of weeks to visit my dad. I'll be glad to get out of here. If you're not here when I get back, I'll know what happened to you."

"What do you mean 'if I'm not here'?"

"Hell, Artie, you know damn well what I mean."

"Oh, Jesus."

PHOENIX HAD TWO daily papers, *The Arizona Republic*, the morning paper, which I delivered, and *The Phoenix Gazette*, the afternoon paper. When I got home, I tore open the *Gazette*. There it was on the front page in a banner headline: **TRUNK MURDERESS ESCAPES ASYLUM**. I read the article feverishly. My mouth felt like a cotton patch.

> PHOENIX, October 21---Winnie Ruth Judd, the cold-blooded killer of her two roommates, broke out of the Arizona State Hospital early this morning, leaving no clue as to her whereabouts. Police began a house-to-house search on the city's east side. The "blond butcher," as she is known, was last seen wearing a white hospital uniform. Mrs. Judd was committed to the hospital in May, 1937 for the 1931 murder of twenty-four year old Hedwig "Sammy" Samuelson and thirty-two year old Agnes Anne LeRoi, and sending their remains to Los Angeles via railroad express. Mrs. Judd is believed to be dangerous and should be approached with extreme caution.

I gobbled up every word of the story, which devoted a paragraph to her escape but mostly recounted the crime. I became more frightened with every word I read, and yet I couldn't stop reading. There was a two-column picture of Winnie Ruth, petite and heartbreakingly beautiful, with bobbed hair and a pouty mouth and a bandage on her hand covering the wound she sustained, apparently, while chopping up her victims.

The *Gazette* continued with a follow-up story of the case on another page, a full eight columns of grisly details that made my legs tremble.

My mother hadn't returned from LA. I wanted her home. I wasn't worried about her because she was with her boss, Rex Alderdice. The truth was that I was afraid to be alone. The balcony off our living room led directly into our apartment and could be scaled easily, so I pulled a chair over to the entrance to the living room---not that it would prevent access, but at least I could hear the chair move if Winnie Ruth tried to enter. I walked over to the front door to make sure it was double locked, then I sat down and finished the rest of the story.

It was gruesome. I could hardly believe that the girl in the picture could do such an awful thing. What bothered me at the time was that the story made me horny. You might think it was weird that the dismemberment of two young, good-looking women by another good-looking woman could have even the slightest element of appeal. Well, for one thing, their relationship was too strange for words. The newspaper account said there were rumors that they were lesbians, but then, in contradiction, there were reports that Winnie Ruth Judd killed the other two women in a jealous rage because all three were after the same guy. Both reports might have been true, but it was something I couldn't reconcile at the time.

As I got further into the story, I learned that Winnie Ruth was no innocent. She was married to a doctor named William Judd who had found employment in Mexico, leaving his wife in Phoenix, where she got a job in a medical clinic. Winnie Ruth had tuberculosis, and Dr. Judd believed the Phoenix climate would be better for her. There she met "Sammy," who also suffered from TB, and Anne. The three became fast friends, "party girls" of a sort, the article said.

While Dr. Judd was in Mexico, the three ladies got to know Jack Halloran, owner of a lumber yard, who had political connections. Halloran was a good-time Charlie; he led a discreet life publicly but was a terror on the sly. He would visit the three girls at night, armed with a big smile and a bottle of booze.

After living together for some time, friction began to develop among the three women, especially after Halloran came on the scene. While Sammy and Anne liked Winnie Ruth, her presence was an irritant to them---a simple matter of two's company, three's a crowd. Or so the paper said. The fact was that Halloran and Winnie Ruth were probably banging each other as I quickly deduced.

The story went on to suggest that she and Halloran, because of their romance, needed their own pad, so Winnie Ruth said goodbye to Sammy and Anne and went off on her own. She still remained friendly with her former roommates. When she moved out, she told them it was because she had found a cheaper place to live.

Sammy and Anne were also fond of the wealthy lumber dealer and resented Winnie Ruth's affair with him, and one time when Winnie Ruth saw him making a play for Anne, an argument erupted between the women. It ended, the newspaper said, in a flurry of bitter words and Winnie Ruth Judd shooting her friends.

That motive, to this day, is a matter of speculation, the paper said. Whatever it was, Jack Halloran was at the center of all the trouble.

In the meantime, in order to dispose of the bodies, Winnie Ruth was said to have dismembered them, stuffing the parts into two trunks and shipping the trunks to the Union Station in Los Angeles. There, according to a plan she had cooked up with her brother, who lived in LA, they would claim the trunks, and then dump them in the Pacific Ocean near Santa Monica. The dismemberment, as far as the story went, occurred only so that she might get the bodies to fit into the trunks. If there had been some maniacal reasons for doing it---something really weird and twisted---it didn't come out in the story.

I was about halfway through the story when I had to stop. I was starting to imagine Winnie Ruth grabbing me in the dark, throwing me down, and with her knife poised over me, stabbing me in the groin, and then---with several swift surgical strokes---dicing my johnson and slitting my throat.

Dear Lord, help me.

I was terrified and horny at the same time. I got up and walked to the front door, tugging it a few times to make sure it was locked. Then I walked over to the porch and looked out into the darkness of McDowell Road. I saw nothing, heard nothing, but was sure that Winnie Ruth Judd was somewhere out there, crouching in the darkness, waiting for me.

I went back to my reading, unable to stop. According to the story, the railway express truck picked up the two trunks and put them on the train to LA. Winnie Ruth followed. When the trunks arrived, they were leaking blood and giving off a horrible odor. At first the baggage handlers believed that someone had killed a deer in Arizona and was shipping the meat to LA. But later, when Winnie Ruth tried to claim the trunks, she was questioned about the contents. The railroad authorities asked that she open them, but she lied and said she was unable to, that her husband had the keys. Skeptical, the railroad authorities called the police. When the trunks were finally opened, they revealed the torso and head of Sammy in one, and the hacked-up parts of Anne in the other. Winnie Ruth Judd was arrested, tried and convicted, and sentenced to death in 1931, long before my arrival in Phoenix.

No one in Phoenix or, for that matter, the rest of the country had much stomach for hanging a woman, the paper said. Winnie Ruth nevertheless remained on Death Row at the state prison in Florence for several years.

Then in 1937, she received another hearing. This time she did a good job of acting insane; her rantings were punctuated by outbursts against Halloran, her former boyfriend, who wanted her out of the way forever. Finally, nearly seven years after the murders, she was adjudged insane and committed to the state hospital in Phoenix, about two miles from my paper route.

When I think of the number of times I rode my bike past the hospital I have to shudder. That hospital was a frightening place, a dark and foreboding building that looked like the workhouse in Oliver Twist---or what I imagined the workhouse looked like. It was set back about fifty yards off Van Buren Street. The windows were vertical in shape with closely spaced bars, and I thought I could make out the faces of some of the inmates peering out from behind them and through the barbed wire.

Winnie Ruth had been sent to the hospital at the same time my mother and I arrived in Phoenix. I had no knowledge of the crime or of her presence at the institution then. One of the faces I saw gazing out of the window could have been hers, but then it could have been the face of my Grandma Dora, straight out of Des Moines, pinched and withered and framed with strands of unkempt hair.

I HARDLY SLEPT at all that night waiting for my mother to come home. I twisted and turned, and even when I began to feel sleepy I wouldn't let sleep happen. I had to keep an eye out for Winnie Ruth. I felt some relief when I heard my mother come in, but then I started thinking about getting up at 5:30 to deliver my papers. It would be dark then and it would mean riding my bike from Central and McDowell over to Twelfth and Pierce, where I got the papers from the circulation truck. Winnie Ruth could be hiding somewhere in the shadows, out of the glare of the streetlights, under a palm tree perhaps: that meant I would have to ride down the center of the streets.

When I did awaken in the morning, my mother was already up, making coffee.

"How was everything?" she asked.

"Fine."

"Any phone calls?"

"Not while I was home."

"Arthur, what's the chair doing in front of the porch door?"

"Nothing," I replied. "There was a lot of noise outside. Some drunks I guess, and I didn't want them climbing up to the porch." I didn't want her to think I was concerned about Winnie Ruth Judd.

She told me about her trip to LA. She said that she and Rex had gone to a regional meeting---something to do with work. She didn't need to explain. I didn't believe her anyway. The two of them had gone to Nogales a few weeks earlier, again supposedly for something work-related. I didn't believe that either. Why would anything concerning the Bureau of Public Debt be discussed in a Mexican border town? What did she take me for, anyhow?

I NOTICED A change in my mother since we had come to Phoenix. No longer the timid, downtrodden soul she was in Des Moines, where she had been doing penance for having married my father, she was now exuding confidence and enjoying herself, living the life that had been denied her, free from the judgmental looks of her relatives, free from Old Jake and all the rest. She was a wage-earner now and self-supporting, if you didn't count the monthly checks she received from her brothers. And most important, she had a friend, a man friend, her boss, Rex Alderdice. Not surprisingly, she was also free of her asthma.

I resented the new Arlene. I didn't know why at the time, but looking back, it made me angry to think she had dragged me away from Des Moines, where I had friends, yanked me out of school, bestowed her problems on me and made me the guilt-ridden accomplice to her mistakes. There would have been no "Poor Arthur" without there having been a "Poor Arlene." And now that I had the Trunk Murderess to contend with, where was Arlene? Making hay in LA and Nogales with her boyfriend.

Some deal.

REX ALDERDICE WAS the regional director of the Bureau of Public Debt. It was an important job, and Rex dressed the part. He wore dark suits and white shirts with too much starch in the collars. Sometimes I thought the collars were choking him because his face would get red and the flesh of his jowls would protrude over the collar, leaving a rim of sweat marks. No one in Phoenix dressed the way Rex did. Jackets and ties were not the usual attire here, but Rex went his own way, and I admired him for it.

As for my mother, I didn't usually think of her in such terms, but there's no doubt she was a good-looking woman---short with auburn hair and a trifle plump. I could see why Rex found her attractive. The most striking thing about them as a couple, though, was the difference in their sizes. Rex was a large man, heavy-set---not fat, just plain big---the kind of man who blocks sidewalks. He had dark hair that was graying at the temples, and that, along with his dark suits and white shirts, made him a distinguished-looking gentleman; a man of authority, not to be trifled with.

I can imagine how our relatives would have responded to the news of my mother's relationship with Rex. I'm sure it would have been disastrous because Rex had two strikes against him. He was a gentile, first of all, and if that wasn't bad enough, he was also a married man with children. His wife, Grace, lived in Phoenix but was often away visiting her own family in Dayton. It must have been a rocky marriage because there was no other explanation for his spending so much time with my mother. At least twice a week he would come for dinner. At other times he came late in the evening, and he and my mother sat on the balcony and talked. I wanted to believe they were just talking, but their groaning and heavy breathing belied that notion.

There were times when Rex came over that I thought about my father. I hadn't seen him since I was a toddler, but from studying his pictures I could tell he was the opposite of Rex Alderdice. My father was a small, wiry man who wore fashionable clothing---early Ivy League style, with narrow knit ties and straight-collar shirts. He must have been self-conscious about his baldness, and he coped with it by wearing snap-brim fedoras, even in his photographs. In them, he was rarely without a cigar. All in all, though, he was only an abstraction in my life, never around Phoenix but off somewhere in the heartland, peddling clothing to the merchants and playing cards. I would have liked to talk with him about Winnie Ruth Judd and my terror-filled nights. I would have liked to talk with someone, anyone but Rex and my mother.

All through the next weeks I grew increasingly frightened of Winnie Ruth. I lost my concentration in school and was depressed, especially when night came. I had now become a diligent reader of *The Republic*, searching for news of her. I often thought about giving up my paper route and getting another job after school. The dark, pre-dawn streets were more than I could deal with.

I wasn't the only one who was frightened. There were a few other boys at PUHS whose mothers kept them in line with threats that Winnie Ruth would chop them into little pieces if they didn't straighten out. Some mothers even kept their kids home from school. Yet, there

I was, braving the early morning darkness, slinging papers at the front doors of houses just a mile or so from the crazy house.

I was pretty desperate that fall of 1939. I knew I had to talk to someone who could help me deal with my fears. But who? Phoenix had only one synagogue, presided over by a reform rabbi, himself a transplanted "lunger" from New York. A classmate at PUHS, Myron Newmark, had told me about the time his parents invited the rabbi and his wife to their home for dinner, preceded by a swim. Myron said the rabbi dove under the water, came up under Myron's legs and rammed his finger into his rectum. The notion of talking to that rabbi, as you can understand, was entirely out of the question.

5

LATE ONE SUNDAY morning, while my mother and Rex were having breakfast at the Westward Ho, I decided to talk with Katherine Antonelli. She would understand. I knocked on her door a few times before she finally answered.

"Who's there?" she called out. I was afraid she might be entertaining a guy she brought home from the restaurant.

"It's me, Arthur."

She unlatched the door, and when she saw me, that knowing smile crossed her lips.

"Well, stranger," she said, pulling her housecoat tight around her body, "to what do I owe the honor?"

"I was just looking to see if Floyd was back," I said, glancing around her living room. The question was stupid because I knew he wasn't.

"Come in, Arthur, sit down. Can I get you coffee, or something?"

"Nothing, thank you." I felt my mouth getting dry.

"Floyd won't be back for a few weeks. Is there something I can do?"

"No, Katherine, I don't think so."

"You're sure?"

Actually, I wasn't sure, I wanted to talk to her about Winnie Ruth. Getting it off my chest was one thing, and another was to have someone tell me that my fears were unfounded. There's no doubt I was going through some lunatic period. A lot of kids my age were breaking out with acne; I was breaking out with *Winnie Ruth vulgaris*, an unmitigated case of horrible fright for which there was no known cure at the drug store. What I didn't dare admit is that I also wanted to see Katherine, to be close to her and feel her warmth.

"Pretty sure," I said finally.

"Well, come sit next to me and tell me what's on your mind."

She sat down on the tattered loveseat and I sat down next to her. I glanced at the unmade bed in the room and at a partially finished glass of wine, The kitchen sink was piled high with dishes. Her brassiere was slung over a kitchen chair. I could feel her thigh pressing against mine. My legs began to shake. I couldn't control the trembling. Dear Lord in heaven, with all your infinite power, don't let me touch her.

"Well, I wanted to..."

"Go ahead, Arthur, say what's on your mind."

"It's not very important, really."

"No?" She looked at me quizzically.

"I think I'd better go."

"Please, Arthur, stay. I've always liked you. Did you know that?"

"Yes."

"I haven't seen much of your mother, now that she's working. How is she?"

"She's fine."

"She has a boyfriend, right, Arthur?"

"Yes."

"Do you like him?"

"He's a good guy."

"I saw him once in the hallway. He's very good-looking."

"Katherine?"

"Yes, what is it Arthur?"

"I think I should go back to my apartment. But I don't really want to. I really came over to find out what you thought about Winnie Ruth's escape. Do you think they'll ever catch her?"

"Why do you care about that? They'll catch her sooner or later. Relax, honey, you're as tight as a banjo string."

She put her arm around me. I could smell the wine on her breath. Her wantonness oozed out of every pore, and I felt like spreading her housecoat apart and burying my head in that wonderful bosom.

Dear God, this woman was my mother's age. What was I thinking? Arthur, you miserable moron, you disgusting piece of garbage. I thought of Floyd, my only true friend in Phoenix. How could I ever face him again, and what if Katherine should tell him? Not on purpose, of course, but what if he should find out? A slip of the tongue and I'd be a certified motherfucker.

And what about Arlene? She and Katherine might get into an argument, and, for spite, Katherine might spill the beans. But there were other things, hideous things, like Old Jake and Uncle Abe renouncing me. I knew Katherine slept with other men, traveling salesmen in town for a few days, men like my father whose only mission was to make out with waitresses like her, men who might unwittingly spread their venereal diseases around like sand in a desert windstorm, and from them to her to me.

Tinkers to Evers to Chance.

Jesus.

She pulled up my sleeve and began stroking my arm, Up and down, up and down, her fingernails gliding lightly over my skin, Oh, Katherine, you big blond voluptuous goddess, I don't really care about any of the things that worry me. I'd risk everything for you. I put my hand under her housecoat and felt her breast. I heard her moan slightly. Then, suddenly, almost without thinking, I jerked my hand away and jumped to my feet.

"I can't, I can't," I heard myself say. "I've got to go." My whole body was shaking. My face was hot with embarrassment.

Katherine stood and faced me. Her housecoat was open. She put her arms around me and kissed me hard on the lips.

"I know, Arthur," she whispered. "I know."

I left her apartment in a daze, walked over to my own apartment and sat down at the breakfast table, lamenting my fate. I know, I know, she had said. What did she know? That I was not a man, not even close to being one? That I was a pygmy next to real men, a frightened, cowering impostor? A real man would have made love to her. He would have faced up to any of the dangers lurking in his mind, and if they came to pass, he would accept his fate like a man. But to back away from possible misfortune, as I had, and not even serious misfortune at that (although try to tell me that at the time) was like being locked up for life in a chicken coop---underscore *chicken*---and waiving any right to a normal life.

And as for Winnie Ruth, there were thousands of people living in Phoenix. Why was it, then, that she was after me, only me? Was it because I wanted her nearly as badly as I wanted Katherine? WINNIE RUTH NABBED IN LOVE NEST WITH FIFTEEN-YEAR-OLD BOY, the headline in *The Republic* would scream. They would read all about it in the *Des Moines Register*. Old Jake would lay down an official curse at B'nai Jesherum and my name would be entered in the Book of Death, right next to my father's, both of us condemned to an eternity in the Pit of Hell.

Suddenly I thought about my bar mitzvah. "Today I am a man," I had said when it was over. I should have added: "but don't be so sure about that." Among the entitlements of being a bar mitzvah boy is the privilege of standing at the *bima* and reading from the Torah, or of being one of the ten men needed to organize and perform in a religious service, But nowhere is it written that you're entitled to be a man in other areas. To take Katherine to bed. Or Winnie Ruth. Or to tell Old

Jake to shove it. Or to have jumped the train in Salina, Kansas, and left my mother free to wheeze through the rest of her life without me.

If I'd had the nerve I would have talked to Rabbi Cohen about this unfortunate hitch in Judaic law. So I speak to you, God: Why is this so? Why the hypocrisy?

TIME PASSED, TWO weeks or so, and I still hung onto my paper route. They hadn't found Winnie Ruth Judd, and my morning dread continued without letup. She was still out there, hiding in the shadows of the palm trees along my paper route, waiting to jump on top of me in the dark. It was early November, the mornings pitch black. One morning at about 6:30, when I was halfway through with my deliveries, I noticed a man sitting on the porch of a house on my paper route. He was wearing a white hospital uniform. I had never seen him before.

"Young man!" he shouted. "Come over here."

I got off my bike and wheeled it up to his front porch. I handed him his paper. Something about him frightened me. I felt my mouth grow dry.

"Yes, sir?"

"I wonder if you could arrange to get here a little earlier," he said. "I have to leave for work soon and I don't have time to read the paper."

The man was short and I could see that he was very muscular. He had a mouthful of uneven teeth. There were tattoos on both arms, one of a serpent's head emerging from a heart, the other of a man's name, which I presumed was his. He had a dark beard, the kind that required a morning and evening shave. He was dressed in white trousers and a white hospital shirt, the kind doctors wore.

"I'll do the best I can, sir." I explained that the routing was up to the carrier supervisor, who decides which blocks come first. "Maybe if I talk to him, he can change my route."

"Oh, heavens, don't bother to do that. Just get here as early as you can." He gave me one of those long, hard-focus stares, his head cocked slightly to the side. He made me nervous as hell. I started to back-pedal toward the sidewalk.

"Wait a minute," he said, "now that I'm on the day shift at the hospital, I'll be seeing more of you. I like to sit on the porch and have my coffee, even though the weather is starting to turn cold. What's your name, young man?"

"Arthur." And then I blurted out: "Which hospital?"

"The Arizona State Hospital. The booby hatch, as you boys probably refer to it. Now tell me, Arthur, what's your whole name?"

"Randall, sir. Are you a doctor?"

"Goodness, no, Arthur. I'm a nurse. I care for the patients. So does my house-mate, Neil. He works the night shift, poor baby. He gets The Gazette. I get The Republic. See how nicely it works out? He's still on duty right now. Would you like to have coffee with me?"

My heart was pounding. I took a deep breath. Why was all this happening to me? First it's Winnie Ruth, now it's a hospital nurse, One way or another, I couldn't avoid being caught up in that house of horror.

"No, sir, I have to finish my deliveries."

"Neil reads The Republic at the hospital," he continued, "and when he gets home he reads The Gazette. Do you deliver The Gazette?"

"N-no," I stammered, "just The Republic."

"Neil and I cross paths for a few hours every day. So we're not apart for too long, just long enough to get lonesome for each other. A little absence is a good thing. Makes the heart grow fonder. Right, Arthur?"

"I guess so," I said, my voice quavering. I had to get away from this creep. I wheeled my bike around and started riding toward the street.

"Wait a minute, young man, not so fast. I'm talking to you."

I braked the bike. I didn't want to be rude and have him report me.

"I want to know where you live and what your phone number is, just in case I miss my paper some morning."

I thought for a moment. I muttered something that sounded like a gurgle.

"Surely you know your phone number?"

I thought quickly, and I said, "We can't give out that information, sir, but if you do miss your paper, call the home delivery department and they'll get one right over to you."

"Can't you bring it over?"

"I go to school," I said.

"Of course you do. I should have known. How old are you, Arthur?"

"Fifteen."

"Just the age when you're interested in girls, right?"

"I guess so."

"Well, be careful. They may look clean, and they make your pencil hard, but do be careful. They spread horrible diseases around."

"I have to go now," I said. I was terrified. I wheeled my bike around. I had a hard time getting my feet in the pedals. The man himself was frightening enough, but what frightened me even more was the thought that he had seen something in me that made him think I was as queer as he was.

"My name is Frank," I heard him call after me. "Frank Girvin. Come see me."

"In a pig's ass," I muttered to myself.

Then and there I made up my mind to quit my paper route. It was bad enough having to deliver papers in the dark with Winnie Ruth still on the loose, but now with this queer after me I couldn't go on any longer. I'd stick it out until I found another route or got a part-time job doing something else. I asked the supervisor the next morning, but he said nothing else was available and that I should be satisfied with what I had. I was sure he was In cahoots with the queer.

The next morning I decided that I'd get to the nurse's house first thing, before he woke up, deliver the Republic and then double-back and finish the rest of my deliveries. That didn't work out, however, because there he was on his porch waiting for me.

"Well, Arthur, you weren't by any chance trying to give me the slip, or were you just so lonesome for me that you had to get here early?"

He caught me off guard. There was nothing I could say. He had me dead to rights, partly anyway. Then, thinking quickly, I said:

"Has there been any news about Winnie Ruth Judd?"

"Strange that you should ask," he replied, nodding his head. "As a matter of fact, she came back to the hospital last night. I'm glad; I missed her so much. Neil called me early this morning and told me. The story should be in the Gazette this afternoon."

It was good news, for sure, and I felt an overwhelming sense of relief, but in a way I was sorry she was caught. I felt strangely sad. I wondered what they would do to her.

"Did the cops catch her?" I asked, timidly.

"Heavens no. The cops could never catch her," he said. "She just walked in, nice as you please. She's a lady, Arthur, not like that trash you see walking down Van Buren."

"Do you know her?"

"Of course I know her. She cuts my hair and Neil's. She washes and sets the women's hair, too. That's how she earns her spending money. She's something, that Ruth."

He stood watching me, leaning against his porch railing, his coffee cup in his hand. His arrogance was smeared across his face, his lips twisted in a wanton smile. This is one evil sonofabitch, I thought. I wanted to ask him other things about her---whether she did weird things with the other patients and was she a nympho lesbian and did she have a dildo and did he ever see her standing naked in the shower. Things like that. My curiosity about her was nearly as great as my fear. As much as I wanted the answers, they'd have to wait. I had to get away from him, One good thing was that I didn't have to worry about Winnie Ruth Judd anymore. She was back at the hospital. Now there was only Girvin to worry about.

I quit my paper route the following day. Winnie Ruth was back in the crazy house and Frank Girvin was out of my life forever. I walked around a free man. After school I began looking for another job. It was the Christmas season. The days were shorter, and nighttime crept in earlier. Lights had been strung up along Central Avenue and downtown on Adams and Washington Streets, The display windows at Goldwaters and Korricks were decorated with Santa Clauses and phony snow. The weather had cooled down but it was still shirtsleeve weather. There were no rosy-cheeked carolers on the street with mufflers over their faces singing "Adeste Fidelis," and that made me a little sad because it made me think of Des Moines. Christmas or not, it was still the desert. You need a vivid imagination to get into the Christmas spirit in Phoenix.

Just a few days before Christmas, however, I got hit with bad news. Winnie Ruth Judd had escaped again. The news came like a kick in the solar plexus. I was stunned. She walked out of the insane asylum like she owned the place. In-one-day, out-the-next. Some Christmas present.

Oh, God, why are you doing this to me?

6

PALM LANE CUTS across Central Avenue four blocks north of McDowell Road. At the time I lived in Phoenix it was the entrance to the world of the early settlers---the privileged and the wealthy. The homes were Spanish-style and spacious, with well-manicured lawns. Even the brutal heat of summer didn't seem to affect the verdant setting. The Salt River Project, which would provide irrigation for the city, was still years away, so the green grass around the homes came at the expense of precious city water and hordes of Mexican laborers.

I rode my bike into the Krakauer's driveway. They lived in a rambling Spanish- style home, filled with expensive furniture, It was only a few blocks from Encanto Park, a forty-acre recreational facility where the Krakauer's two children often played under the watchful eye of a live-in babysitter.

It was a warm Sunday in January, and my mother and I had been invited for an afternoon picnic and swim. You had to come from hearty stock to handle the cold water in the pool, but a few guests were already swimming when I arrived, among them Rabbi Cohen. When he saw me, he beckoned furiously for me to jump in the pool. I shook my head just as furiously. I remembered Myron Newmark's story about the Rabbi and his hair-trigger middle finger.

My mother was already there when I arrived. Another guest had brought her. I was glad I rode my bike over because I could leave whenever I liked. I would have been able, if I had the courage, to deal with my mother's anger had I done so.

My mother saw a great deal of the Krakauers. She had been introduced to them by a friend who had come to Phoenix from Des Moines. They had a lot of money, and probably were under the impression that my mother did, too, my mother being the gifted actress she was. The Krakauer family consisted of the father, Arnold, his wife, Dorothy, and their two children, Kyle and Elizabeth. I didn't like any of them, chiefly because I wasn't comfortable around reform Jews. I remembered the self- satisfied looks on the faces of the reform Jews in Des Moines, suggesting they had special hides worthy of divine protection. The Krakauers had the same arrogant smirks. Now I don't discount the fact that I had a huge chip on my shoulder and probably read too much into their treatment of me, even though the Krakauers, for a time at least, regarded me as the wealthy son of Arlene Randall. How could they have known that the real Arthur Randall had lived as a beggar all his life in someone else's home and, what's more, was the son of Ben Randall.

Arnold Krakauer was a jovial man controlled by his wife, who reminded me of Alicia Baldwin, my teacher at Kenilworth school. She had a hook nose and silky blonde hair and a self-important air---a self-assured woman to whom no harm would ever come. If I had asked her if she thought the cops would ever catch Winnie Ruth Judd, she wouldn't have known what I was talking about. What's more, if Winnie Ruth had sneaked up behind her and thrown her to the ground, a knife poised at her throat, Dorothy Krakauer would have chilled her with a withering glance and sent her slinking back to the state hospital.

When I arrived, my mother was busy helping Dorothy Krakauer with supper, and the two Krakauer children began tugging at me to play croquet. I thought they were little turds, and Floyd would have agreed if he had been there. I freed myself and walked over to pay my respects to the rabbi and his wife.

No matter what the rabbi said or did to maintain his exalted position as leader of the reform Jews of Phoenix, I could never forget that he goosed Myron Newmark: that one act brought him down to the level of Frank Girvin. I thought about the statues in the park, the ones with all the generals and public figures sitting on their horses. If the horses had all four legs on the ground, the man on the horse was not a warrior. But, watch out, it the rider was a warrior the two front legs of the horse were raised, indicating that the horse was in the throes of battle. Why shouldn't statues of rabbis be depicted along the same lines? Those who faithfully followed the precepts of Judaism would be depicted in solemn prayer, and those like Rabbi Cohen could be shown with their right hands raised out of the folds of their robes, their middle fingers pointed not toward the Torah but to the dark midnight of some kid's rectum.

After supper I wanted to go home, but Dorothy Krakauer wouldn't hear of it. Kyle and Elizabeth wanted me to stay overnight, she said. They simply adored me, she told my mother.

"I have to get to school early," I muttered. It was a weak and unconvincing excuse.

"Now, Arthur, that's a lovely invitation," my mother said. "After all those months getting up early to deliver papers, I wouldn't think It would hurt you to get up a little earlier this one time."

I was boxed in, betrayed by my mother and her social aspirations.

I didn't relish the idea of being alone with Dorothy Krakauer. One time, when my mother went to Los Angeles with Rex Alderdice, I had been at the Krakauers for a pre-arranged dinner. Dorothy put me under the grill-light, bombarding me with questions. I recalled our conversation vividly:

"Your mother is in Los Angeles, is she? I love it there. I hope she has fun. She works so hard."

"I guess she does," I replied.

"When will she back?"

"Tomorrow, I think."

"I know your parents are divorced. It must be hard on you not having a father around."

I remember feeling uneasy. I wasn't sure what she knew or didn't know, or what she was leading up to. "It's not so bad." I said.

"I mean not having any brothers or sisters."

"I get along okay."

Then she said, "Do you ever see your father?"

"Pardon?"

She had momentarily caught me off guard.

"Your father... do you ever see him?"

I hesitated. "I haven't for a while, but he writes to me a lot, a whole lot." The truth was, I hadn't heard from my father since we left Des Moines.

"You must want to see him very badly. Boys your age need a father around. It's important for a lot of reasons."

"I guess so," I said. I was sure now that her questions were not just an attempt to make conversation. She was a clever woman, and she was trying to lead me into some kind of trap.

"You are a fortunate young man, Arthur. Yes you are," she said, her head bobbing up and down to emphasize her point. "Your mother is a wonderful woman, just wonderful."

I had the feeling that all this was getting around to Rex Alderdice, but I wasn't sure. I didn't know if the Krakauers knew about Rex and if my mother had told Dorothy Krakauer that she was going to LA with him. No matter. I'd be damned if she'd get anything out of me, and I didn't like being forced to cover up for my mother. Why hadn't she told me what to say, since it was she who arranged for me to be at the Krakauers.

"Your mother is so pleasant and outgoing," she continued. "I'm very happy for her. She's made so many friends here---women with whom she can share a lovely trip to California." Then she said, as she cocked her head to one side: "Do I know the lady she went with? I do wish they'd have invited me. I love California."

"She went with a lady in our building," I said, trying not to sound too curt. "Her name is Katherine Antonelli. She's real nice."

I HEARD THE latch snap on a closet door and awakened from a sound sleep. I had been sleeping in a spare room off the Krakauer's patio. As I looked around, the moonlight streaming into the room, I saw Dorothy Krakauer standing naked in front of the clothes closet. I could make out her white body, the triangular patch of black above her legs, and her sharp pointed breasts, as sharp as her hawk's nose. Her breasts jutted out in the shape of the college pennants I had seen decorating the walls of Mickey Rooney's room in *Love Comes To Andy Hardy*.

She was posing in front of the full-length mirror on the closet door, adjusting the position of the door from time to time in order to get the fullest illumination of the moonlight on her body-- a moon-gilded vision admiring her reflection. I was certain she knew I was watching her. I had never seen a woman naked before, a woman nearly my mother's age, and I wasn't sure whether it would be permissible to feast my eyes on her or whether I should turn away and bury my head in the pillow. I thought that if I continued to look at her, I might go blind.

A few moments later, I removed the pillow from my face to see if she was still there, and---*Oh, Jesus, dear Lord*---there in the mirror was another reflection. It was not Dorothy Krakauer but another woman, and she was naked too.

This woman had bobbed hair and features softer and rounder than Dorothy Krakauer's. She had full lips that turned down into a pout.

Lying crumpled at her feet was a hospital gown. In her hand was a hatchet whose steel blade caught a ray of moonlight and shone like a fizzled comet. I caught a glimpse of a bandage on her right hand.

She was the most beautiful woman I had ever seen, more beautiful even than Katherine Antonelli. I wiped my eyes, hoping I could rub away the apparition. It didn't disappear. I was certain I was losing my mind. *Oh, Lord, why do you keep doing this to me?* I pushed my head deep into my pillow and screamed as loud as I could, the pillow barely muffling my sobs,

A few moments later I lifted my head and glanced toward the closet. The other woman had disappeared. In her place I saw Dorothy Krakauer, still admiring her reflection in the mirror. She pulled a bathrobe off a hanger, draped it over her shoulders and tied the belt loosely around her waist, leaving her hands free. She moved them slowly over her body, shot a glance in my direction and then left the room.

7

I WALKED INTO WESTERFIELD'S Drug Store on a Friday afternoon late in January in answer to an ad that appeared in the Help Wanted column of the Republic. The job was for a part-time delivery boy who could also do cleanup work behind the soda fountain.

Norman Westerfield, the pharmacist who owned the store, was filling prescriptions behind the counter. He glanced down at me. I told him I was answering the ad in the Republic.

"Do you have a bike, kid?"

"Yes, sir."

"We deliver all over town," he said. "If you don't know your way around, I can't use you."

"I know my way around. I've lived here nearly three years, and I've had a paper route ever since we moved here. I know all the streets pretty well."

He pushed aside his work and looked me over. "We'll find out soon enough."

He was a tall man, standing slightly bent over. He wore a white lab coat over a blue sport shirt. His thinning blond hair was combed to the side in a vain attempt to conceal his baldness. He handed me an application.

"Here, fill this out and give it back to me. At least we'll find out if you can read and write."

When I finished filling out the form, I handed it back to him and watched nervously as he scowled at my answers, Then, turning his back to me, he made a phone call. I assumed it was to PUHS. "I'm trying to get some information on one of your students," I overheard him say, "an Arthur Randall. That's right, Randall... a sophomore... class of 1942, so he says. Attendance record, grades, that sort of thing..."

I fidgeted as he talked, sure that the school was giving him an earful of all my transgressions. I strolled around the store. It had a long soda fountain, fifteen stools in all. There were three long gondolas running the length of the store and stocked with more lotions and beauty preparations than I knew existed. I remembered thinking that this was one job I had to have.

Westerfield finally beckoned to me. "I think I'll try you out," he said, as I approached. "They seem to think a good deal of you at the high school, but it won't be any picnic around here like PUHS is, I'll tell you that. Give me a good day's work, that's all I ask. I don't coddle my employees, just ask them. If I catch you loafing or goofing around, you'll be out on your ass in short order. Understand?"

"Yes, sir."

"Make sure you do. First thing, can the Mr. Westerfield. Call me Norm. We're all family here. Second thing, if there's something you don't understand, don't be afraid to ask questions. Even the stupid ones are okay---just don't ask the same stupid question more than ten times. Got me?"

"Yes, Norm."

"The pay is thirty-five cents an hour. I'd like you to work after school for a couple of hours, and then a full day on Saturday. Sunday we're closed, so don't come in."

"What kind of work do I do?" I asked.

"Everything you're asked to do, but mainly you'll be doing odd jobs at the soda fountain between deliveries---washing dishes and glasses, sweeping the floor and keeping the counter clean. Maybe you'll be drawing cokes and phosphates when things get real busy, but that depends on Hooks. Marvin Hooks runs the fountain, and he'll show you the ropes.

"Another thing, kid: Tips at the counter go into the tip jar and get divided equally at the end of the day. You get no share, but delivery tips are all yours. You'll find it's a better deal. One more thing: everyone behind the counter wears a white apron and white cap---an overseas cap, they used to call them, or a field cap. Take your pick. Hooks will show you. Do you know what an overseas cap is?"

"I don't think so," I said.

"Then I guess you didn't serve in the army, eh, kid?" He laughed at his joke.

"I wasn't even born," I replied.

"I know, I know," he said. "How about your daddy, did he fight?"

"Yes," I answered, "he was in France."

"Then you come from good stock. I served, too, at Fort Leavenworth, Kansas. I fought the whole war there, pushing pills, same as I'm doing now. We didn't wear overseas caps at Leavenworth. We wore garrison caps. Do you know what they are?"

"No, Norm,"

"They have round flat crowns and a leather visor. Standard issue if you were based stateside, like I was. Your daddy wore an overseas cap like the one you'll be wearing. Look over at Hooks behind the fountain. That's an overseas cap."

I turned to look at the man behind the fountain. He was a skinny, scowling little man with a barrel chest. The sleeves of his white shirt were rolled up tight, as high as his underarms would permit. His skinny arms had protruding veins. They looked like sash cords had been implanted under the skin. I disliked him on sight.

"I have a picture of my father wearing a cap like that," I said to the druggist, but he had already turned his attention back to his work.

"You'd better get out of here now, I'm busy. Be back here Monday at four o'clock. Don't be late. Monday's a busy delivery day."

I left the store, elated, but I had some misgivings about Hooks.

WHEN I REPORTED for work the following Monday, I was a half hour early. Arlene said I'd make a good impression by showing up ahead of time. She was right. I could tell Norm was pleased.

When he saw me, Hooks came over and shoved a cap and apron at me, and told me to walk behind the soda fountain and look things over. I inspected the fountain supplies: the ice cream bins, one for each of the five flavors offered by the store; the glass jar holding the marshmallow topping; the different flavors of syrup in their stainless steel dispensers; and a large container of Horlick's malt flanked on either side by two high speed mixers.

From behind the fountain I could look out over the entire store---the prescription department just to the left of the fountain, the magazine rack at the other end. Presently, Norm walked over.

"Arthur," he said, "I want to give you a quick lesson in retailing. I want you to be alert for shoplifters. When we lose merchandise to some goddamn thief, it's murder. We're out what the merchandise costs us plus the profit we make from the sale. What I'm asking you to do is to be on the lookout for thieves, but don't confront them yourself---report what you see to me or to Hooks, and do it fast. Okay?"

I was flattered that Norm was taking me into his confidence and treating me as an adult.

"Okay, Norm."

"Lesson number two. The soda fountain is the crown jewel of the store. The stuff on the counters and the prescriptions pay the rent but the fountain is what brings in customers. So we want to be extra nice to our fountain patrons. Give 'em plenty of service and kiss their asses from here to Casa Grande..."

"Even if they ask for seconds?"

"Well, that's a matter of judgment. You won't be put in that position because you'll be doing Cokes and phosphates, but I'd say it depends on the customer. If it's a young lady with a nice smile and big tits, give it to her, but only half a glass."

A radio played non-stop on a shelf behind the fountain. As I was soon to find out, the drug store was a neighborhood gathering place. Customers could sip their sodas while catching snatches of *Helen Trent* or *Our Gal Sunday*. On those Friday nights when there was a big fight at Madison Square Garden, Norm would keep the fountain open late so that some of the regulars could come in and listen to the Brown Bomber demolishing Paulino Uzcudun or Arturo Godoy or big Abe Simon. On those nights, Norm would ask me to stay a little later, and he'd slip me half-a-buck.

Seating at the fountain was at a premium. The customers who had to wait for a seat would usually stroll over to the magazine rack and leaf through the pages of *Coronet, Saturday Evening Post*, and Street & Smith's *Dime Sports* and *Dime Detective*. Norm didn't mind if customers read the magazines as long as they didn't do it for too long, and in so doing kill a sale. In those cases, he'd walk over and in a nice way ask them for their library card. But when customers took their magazines to the counter to become stained with drippings from their chocolate sundaes, they were politely asked to pay for them.

The policy was strictly enforced by Hooks. He was an ex-short-order cook from Oklahoma who had come to Phoenix for his asthma and emphysema. He was loyal only to the man who paid his salary but bullied me and the two part-time women who rotated hours behind the counter. "A spoiled sheeny, helpless as a baby," is how he described me to Norm.

Between deliveries, I washed glasses and wiped the counter clean. If I was caught up on my chores and there were no deliveries, I could wait on customers, but I was limited to drawing cokes, Green Rivers and phosphates, drinks that Hooks felt comfortable entrusting to me. But if the fountain was busy and Hooks and one of the girls were backed up on orders for shakes and sundaes---the more elaborate concoctions--- they might assign one of the orders to me. Even then, I was not allowed to serve the finished product directly to the customers until it was first presented for inspection to Hooks or to a girl on duty.

For the first few weeks on the job, I couldn't believe my good fortune. I liked working in the store. I liked Norm Westerfield, and I couldn't wait for Floyd to come back from Salt Lake City so he could see where I worked. He'd be jealous as hell, in view of all the good things about the job; even Hooks, who complained endlessly about me, had become only an annoyance. The counter was never clean enough. Or there were lipstick stains on the glasses, stains that couldn't be detected by any other human eye except his. When it seemed as if he had run out of things to complain about he'd manage to come through with a killer complaint: a beef about the spoons not being clean enough, or being full of soap film, or not having the sparkle they had before I came on the job. There was no pleasing him. His chronic complaining didn't bother me as much as his ear-shattering voice and foul mouth.

One time when the counter was jammed with customers and I was busy whipping up a chocolate milk shake, Hooks grabbed my arm, nearly knocking the mixing canister out of my hand. "Look, you weakling," he shouted, "when you press down on the syrup dispenser, push the pump in all the way, all the way down till you hit bottom." He grabbed the canister out of my hand, and placing it in front of the chocolate dispenser, pushed down hard on the pump. Then, once the pump wouldn't go any farther, he released it, the sweet brown syrup now bursting forth like an oil gusher.

"The dispenser is calibrated for portion control," he lectured me and anyone else within earshot, "and if you weren't up all night playing with yourself you'd have the goddamn strength to give the customers their money's worth."

I felt a red flush creeping up my neck. I wanted to dump the mixing can on top of Hooks's head, but he had already served It to a customer. I wouldn't have done it anyway, no matter how angry I was. There were a few snickers at the counter, but most customers turned their heads away, embarrassed for me.

Later, Westerfield came over. "Don't take Marvin too seriously," he said. "He gets in these moods. Do what he says, but don't pay any attention to him, if you get what I mean." He smiled and gave me a good-natured poke on the arm.

One day, in the late afternoon, just as I was about to go off duty, I noticed a girl at the counter. I had been busy washing glasses, and she was waiting to place her order. I walked over to her.

"May I have a chocolate sundae, please," she said. I had seen her before at PUHS. She was a pretty girl with dark hair and fair skin, maybe a year or two older than me. She wore a white sweater and a dark grey skirt, and I could see the full outline of her breasts pressed against the counter.

"One chocolate sundae, coming up," I said.

I kept my eyes fastened on her breasts as I scooped vanilla ice cream into the dish. I had seen her hanging around the hallways with some hot-shot seniors and figured she had either just graduated or was in her senior year. I had recently become infatuated with a few girls at school, but never let on about it. I was afraid of their indifference, perhaps even of their contempt if they ever found out. Anyway, they probably had me figured as being a "briefcase Billy" who didn't have time for girls, or didn't care about them. In fact, I had once been infatuated with the girl at the counter, this very same one, and had searched the hallways just for a glimpse of her pretty face and big breasts. I was lucky she hadn't come into the store when Hooks went into his tirade and accused me of pulling my pud.

I placed the sundae in front of her. She smiled at me, a very sweet smile.

"You're new here aren't you," she said, as she studied my face. "I haven't seen you before, have I?"

"I started about three weeks ago, just part-time after school. I've seen a lot of you at school, though."

"I sort of thought I'd seen you before, too. What grade are you in?"

"Just a sophomore. How about you? Are you a senior?"

"Not anymore, lucky me. I'm graduating this February, barely."

"What do you mean, 'barely'?"

"I mean I'm a long way from being valedictorian, as far away as you can get."

"I don't know about that," I said. "I'll bet you're pretty smart."

"Well, thank you, kind sir."

"I think I saw you hanging around with Phil Karrick and Buster Neff, that gang from varsity football, right?"

"You're pretty observant, aren't you, mister what's-your-name?"

"Arthur, Arthur Randall," I replied.

"Hi, Arthur," she said, flashing her pretty smile. "I'm Myrna Handmacher,"

"Hi, Myrna." I watched as she took her first spoonful of the sundae. "How is it?" I asked."

"Not bad," she said, "not half bad. I love the sundaes here."

"The chocolate syrup dispenser is calibrated so that you get a big helping of chocolate, bigger than most places. That's what makes ours special, plenty of chocolate."

"I haven't the slightest idea what calibrated means, but if you say so, Arthur, it's probably true." She took another spoonful of her sundae. And then she said, "You don't mind if I call you something besides Arthur, do you?"

No girl had ever engaged me in conversation before unless she wanted my help on an English or History test. I wanted to keep the conversation going, but I was afraid she'd catch me staring at her breasts and stomp out in a huff. I wondered if Norm would mind if I offered her seconds, just to get her to stick around. The size of her tits certainly warranted it.

"I don't mind. There's this friend of mine---he calls me Artie."

"Well, I don't like 'Arthur,' it sounds too stiff. And I don't much like 'Artie' either, it sounds too baby-ish. You know what?" she said, staring hard at my face and then slowly nodding. "I think that, deep-down, you're really an Arturo. Yes, yes, you're an Arturo. Does that sound silly?"

"Gosh, no, Myrna."

"Good, well from now on I'll call you Arturo. It's more romantic than Artie, and I have a feeling you're very romantic."

Very softly, so that only she could hear, I began to sing, "*She's a Latin from Manhattan / She's a Forty-second Streeter...*" As soon as I sang the words I regretted it. I was making fun of her for having paid me a compliment. It was only because I was nervous, I told myself. I hated myself. I hated my big smart-aleck mouth. *Please forgive me, Myrna.*

"What was that song, Arturo?"

"Oh that, just some dumb thing I heard on the radio."

"Arturo?"

"Yes"

"That friend you were telling me about, the one who calls you Artie, you two must have fun together."

"Yeah, we do, we kid around a lot."

"Do I know him?"

"I don't think so," I said. "He lives in the same apartment building I do. He used to go to PUHS, but not anymore."

She shrugged.

I watched her as she finished her sundae, noticing how delicately she wiped away the chocolate smudges at the corners of her mouth.

"I sure missed these lately," she said. "I gotta make up for lost time. I'm usually here a few times a week."

"I must have missed you. I guess I was out making deliveries."

"My folks took me back east over New Year's. That's probably why you haven't seen me."

"Where back east? I asked.

"Kansas City. We used to live there. My grandparents are there."

"I'm from Des Moines," I said. "That's not far from Kansas City, is it?"

"I don't think it is."

"That's good. I'll look you up next time I'm in Des Moines and you're in Kansas City."

Laughing, she reached across the counter and placed her hand on my arm. And then she said, "Why, Arturo, you don't have to wait that long." She slipped off the stool and left the store. I stared after her, a funny feeling in the pit of my stomach.

PHOENIX WAS UNSEASONABLY warm for late January, over 90-degrees for the seventh day in a row. The big overhead fans in the store made the heat bearable but did little to curb the thirst of the fountain regulars. They surged into the store and stood impatiently, one and two deep, behind each stool. I was pressed into emergency service at the expense of making prompt prescription deliveries. "Hold off on all deliveries," Norm said, "all but the critical medications." The best news was that, because of the sudden rush, I could make all the elaborate creations without having them inspected first.

The fountain was still jammed at six in the evening. I knew I'd be asked to work late. I was tired. The only chance I had to sit down was on my bike when I made the important deliveries. Customers filed in and out so fast that they became a faceless blur, all of them hot and thirsty.

It was while I was busy wiping the counter, a wet dish rag in one hand and dirty glasses in the other, that I felt a hand grabbing my wrist, the hand coming from someone at the counter. I looked up and noticed first a hairy arm, then a tattoo of a coiled serpent slithering down from the short sleeves of the man's white hospital uniform. I found myself staring into the face of the nurse from the insane asylum, the man's jagged teeth jutting out like truncated spikes. At that moment it was as if a sharp chill had blown through the store and into my heart like an Apache's deadly arrow.

It was Frank Girvin. I hadn't seen him in weeks, and now he had slipped onto a vacant stool and back into my life. I knew my job could turn sour fast, now that he knew where I worked. I realized I'd be at his mercy as long as I worked at the drug store. Girvin, that weirdo creep. I cursed my miserable luck. Winnie Ruth Judd was still on the loose, and now Girvin had drawn a bead on me.

Jesus, why don't they let me alone?

"Hey, Randall, get movin', move your sheeny ass." All at once another assault, this time from Hooks, Hooks in one of his frenzies. "C'mon, jagoff, get those glasses off the counter. We're running short."

Girvin, still smiling, slowly released his grip on my arm, then bent forward on the counter, his face next to mine. "Tell him to go fuck himself, Arthur. Do it," he hissed, "do it now."

For a moment I thought Girvin had suddenly become my ally. I looked hopefully into the nurse's face, saw his grin widen, the snaggled teeth glinting wickedly, the eyes cruel and taunting. Then, for no reason, I thought about a movie I had seen at the Orpheum, the one where Randolph Scott was leading a wagon train of settlers across the plains. Indians from every direction, their painted faces frozen in hideous leers, came thundering out of the hills, unleashing volley after volley of arrows at the hapless settlers. Standing in the midst of the battle, egging on the Indians, were two white men, one wearing a white nurse's uniform and waving his arms frantically, the other a barrel-chested Okie with sinewy arms, blowing a cavalry charge on a bugle.

"Arthur," Girvin said, snapping his fingers in front of my face, "I'm talking to you. I would like a phosphate."

"Yes, sir," I said, stifling an urge to cry.

"Make it a cherry phosphate. You do have a cherry, don't you?"

I pretended not to have heard. Feigning nonchalance, I put ice in a glass, pumped in cherry syrup and simple syrup, and filled the glass with carbonated water, trying my best to avoid looking at Girvin. My hands were trembling, and I accidentally tipped over the phosphate glass as I placed in on the counter. The sweet red liquid flooded the counter and spilled onto Girvin's lap. He jumped off his stool and began brushing his white hospital pants. "This goddamn stuff stains!" he yelled.

Now Hooks began screaming at me, "You clumsy little sheeny. Wipe that stuff up and give the customer a clean towel. I'm gonna have Norm get rid of you. Nobody works for me who can't put a glass down on the counter straight. Nobody."

"I'm sorry," I said, and was ashamed of myself for having said it. Girvin stood by his stool, listening gleefully as Hooks continued his tirade.

"If you get fired," he said to me, "I'll help you get your paper route back. Then I won't have to travel so far to see you, will I?"

He flashed me an insinuating smile and walked toward the door. Before leaving the store, he turned back toward me and with his fingers spread apart pretended to be brushing dry the damp area of his trousers. He called out: "Hasta luego, Arthur, I'll see you later."

8

IT WAS NEARLY quitting time, and as soon as I cleaned up the counter I could go home. I wanted to get as far away from the drugstore as I could. Maybe do nothing when I got there but sit around and listen to the radio. Arlene would be there, and I'd feel better with her around. After all, she was my mother, although she was the last person I could talk to---about Girvin, or Hooks, or Winnie Ruth Judd, or anything else for that matter. I had never talked with her before about anything personal---never, not about what was going on with her and Rex, not about her divorce from my father, and not about why my father had never come to see me. I had questions, hundreds of them, one heaped on top of the other, none of them ever asked, many of them never even formed.

Even if I had been able to ask them, Arlene would never understand how such questions could pop into my mind. Hadn't she worked and sacrificed, just for me? And shouldn't I be grateful for everything she had done? We had our own place to live and there was plenty of food on the table, wasn't that enough? Why should she have to answer questions, too? I knew the script by heart. I had plenty of years to memorize it. If I told her that I was scared most of the time---scared of Winnie Ruth, scared of Girvin, scared of Hooks, she'd never understand. She'd only get annoyed and accuse me of deliberately bringing it up just to make her life miserable.

I said good-bye to Norm and rode my bike back to my apartment. I couldn't get Girvin out of my mind. I was sure he'd come back to the drugstore now that he knew where I worked. I wanted him to leave Phoenix and get a job at another crazy house somewhere. And if he didn't go away, maybe he'd have a heart attack and die. And if he didn't die on his own, then maybe I could help him die. It wouldn't be very hard, I'd put poison in his cherry phosphate, and stand behind the counter looking innocent while his face turned to a reddish purple and he'd start clutching at his throat, gasping for breath. Finally he'd look pleadingly into my eyes for help, but I would just stand there, unconcerned, my lips casually forming the words "fuck you" and delivering them so silently and subtly that none of the onlookers could make them out. As his last desperate act, he would look up to his God, his last court of appeal, the pain in his stomach excruciating, then he would bend over and, emitting one final gasp, drop in his tracks. But in that final instant, with death seconds away, he would realize that he had made one hell of a mistake pushing Arthur Randall around.

I shook my head, trying to clear away the reverie. I shouldn't be thinking this way. I could never kill anyone, not even Girvin. Most likely Girvin would be part of my life as long as we both lived in Phoenix. Even if I quit my job at the drugstore, Girvin would find me. I was trapped. There was no escaping him; there was nowhere I could go. Make him die, dear Lord, I prayed, make him leave me alone.

But it wasn't only Girvin, I reminded myself. There was also Winnie Ruth and Marvin Hooks and Rabbi Cohen and Dorothy Krakauer. I hated them all. They were encircling me, ready to close in. Winnie Ruth would have her murderous butcher knife in her hand, ready to lop off my johnson. Marvin Hooks would have an armload of mixing cans ready to bounce off my skull, and Rabbi Cohen, his middle finger extended, would be about to shove it in my rectum. I thought I would cave in from the strain.

I told Floyd about Girvin the next day. It was Sunday. Katherine was home, lounging around in her housecoat. She kissed me on the cheek when she saw me, just as if nothing had gone on between us. If Floyd hadn't been in the room, I would have ripped off her housecoat and buried my head in her bosom. Anyway, I think that's what I'd have done.

"So who is this guy, anyway?" Floyd asked once we had left his apartment.

"I told you all I know," I said. "He's some kind of a queer and he works at the crazy house and he's chasing me."

"Yeah, yeah, but what's his angle? Why is he after you? There are plenty of guys around with fatter butts than yours, Artie."

"C'mon, Floyd, be serious,"

"I am serious. I'm looking for a motive."

"Sure, sure. Charlie Chan, Honolulu police department."

"Listen to me, Artie, I have a theory. If you let him have it, he won't bother you anymore."

"You're crazy, Floyd."

"I don't mean 'let him have *it*', I mean 'let him *have* it'... you know, *rat-a-tat-tat*. That kind of 'let him have it.'" Floyd pretended to be holding a machine gun and spraying me with a torrent of bullets.

"I'm glad you cleared that up," I said.

"Floyd said: "He's just another pansy, and he's picking on you because he knows you're scared shitless. Am I right?"

"I guess so." There wasn't much conviction in my voice.

"Okay. How about my bringing in a couple of torpedoes from New York. Swarthy guys in tight-fitting overcoats with bulges under their coats, snap brim hats..."

"Jesus, Floyd, you're at it again."

"Just listen, Artie. It's dark outside. The powerful closed car comes roaring around the corner, tires screeching. They spot Girvin. Two guns are extended from the car's window. *Rat-a-tat-tat-tat.* Girvin falls over dead, the blood flowing freely from the holes in his bullet-riddled body..."

"What's that from?"

"Something I saw at the Orpheum---*Little Tough Guy*, I think."

"Thanks, Floyd, I knew I could count on you."

"I'll be serious, Artie, Forget about that guy. He's just raggin' you. He's all bushwah."

I CONTINUED WORKING at the drugstore through the rest of the winter. Girvin hadn't appeared, and my apprehension about having another encounter with him eased off. Myrna dropped in only once in the past six weeks. I had been sweeping the floor behind the counter when I saw her.

"Hi, Myrna." My heart was pounding.

She gave me a big smile. "Hi, Arturo." She was carrying several books, and she was wearing a tan cardigan sweater and a gray skirt, and her hair looked longer than it did in January. She was even prettier than I remembered.

"How was graduation?" I said.

"I got my diploma. My parents were happy and I was happy. End of story."

"I haven't seen you in a long time. Did you find a place with better sundaes than ours?"

"Don't be silly, Arturo."

"Okay, then, how about my making you the usual?"

"Absolutely. My mother tells me I'm a creature of habit. A girl has to listen to her mother, right, Arturo?"

"Well, not always," I said, wondering where I had gotten the courage for such banter.

"Why, Arturo, what do you mean?"

I quickly began making her chocolate sundae, turning my full attention to the task. I knew I was blushing, and hoped she wouldn't notice.

"Nothing, really. I didn't mean anything."

Myrna smiled and leaned over the counter, her large bosom directly in my gaze. "I think you did. You did, didn't you?"

"Did what...?"

"Mean something by your remark---you know, that a girl shouldn't always listen to her mother."

"Honest, I didn't," I stammered. "Honest to God."

"You know what I think, Arturo? I think you were trying to get sexy with me. Were you?"

"No, Myrna," I replied, "honest,"

"Then I guess that means you don't think I'm attractive."

"No, no, I think you're the best looking girl I ever met."

"Do you really?"

"Yes."

"Do you tell other girls that'?"

"No," I declared, "never. I don't know any other girls, Myrna, not like you."

"I don't know about that," she said. "I'll bet you've got dozens of girls, all kinds."

"I told you I don't."

She began singing: *"You can't pull the wool over my eyes / You can't get away telling those lies..."*

"What's that?"

"Just a song," she said. "Helen Ward sings it."

"You still think I'm kidding you, don't you?"

"Yes, I do," she said. "I think all boys are the same. They never tell you the truth."

"I'd never lie to you, Myrna, never."

"Maybe you wouldn't, but the boy I go out with now, he would."

"Who is he? Do I know him?"

"Maybe. Maybe not."

"Well, tell me his name."

"No," she said.

"Does he go to PUHS? You can tell me that, can't you?"

"Yes, he did at one time, but he got kicked out, and that's all I'm saying."

"It serves him right."

I moved away from where she was sitting to wait on another customer. Hooks was not around and I had to tackle a banana split, the first one I ever made. When I finished, I passed it by Myrna for her approval. She gave me an okay sign and I placed it before the customer. The customer looked pleased, and I returned to where Myrna was seated. And then she said: "Why did you say 'it serves him right'?"

"It serves him right because he goes out with you, that's why."

"Arturo!" she exclaimed. "You're jealous, aren't you?"

"Heck, no," I said.

"Heck, yes, is what you mean."

"So what if I am?" I said.

"Then you admit it. Oh, Arturo, I wish you were a year or two older."

"Your boyfriend, whatever his name is, is he a year or two older?"

"Yes, and I'm not saying anymore, either."

I shrugged. Then, for the first time, I noticed the books she was carrying. She had placed them on the counter when she first walked in. I peered at the titles. One was *Vanity Fair*, the other a textbook on advanced geometry.

"Don't you think Thackeray is great, Myrna?"

"No, he's boring."

"Then why are you reading him?"

"It's this damn course I'm taking."

"Where?"

"Arizona State. They're required. I have to take them to enroll in the Fall."

"You didn't tell me," I said.

"There's lots I don't tell you," she said.

"I'm sure that's true."

"Now what does that mean?"

"Nothing."

"You are jealous, Arturo, insanely, madly jealous." She put one hand on her hip, fluttered her eyelids and with her other hand outstretched pretended to be holding a cigarette.

"So what if I am, Bette Davis?"

"I just love boys who are jealous of me..."

"All boys?"

She pushed aside her empty dish and grabbed her books. She leaned over the counter, her bosom resting on the countertop, and kissed me squarely on the lips. "Not all boys, Arturo," she said as she turned and walked away, "just you."

I stood gazing after her, her gray skirt clinging temptingly to her body as she walked out of the store.

WINNIE RUTH JUDD had disappeared from the hospital nearly four months before. In that time, nights had become very hard for me. There had been no sign of her, not even the usual false spotting reports. Neither The Republic nor The Gazette had run any follow-up stories on her. The fact that she was nowhere to be found didn't allay my fears but rather intensified them. The suspense was awful. As far as I was concerned, she was even more dangerous by not tipping her hand but quietly plotting more atrocities, waiting patiently in the dark to pounce on some unsuspecting victim——namely, me. There was always the feeling that she was going to grab me in the dark.

It suddenly occurred to me that she was being harbored by someone. She couldn't be roaming around without food, without a roof over her head, without some kind of help from someone. Somebody was sheltering her, feeding and doing even God-knows-what to her. It was too painful to think about. My mind then turned to Girvin. He was her benefactor. I was sure of it. Hadn't he said he was her friend, that he liked her, that she even cut his hair? And hadn't he said that the cops would never catch her? There had to be a connection between the two of them. What better hideout than in Girvin's home? No one would ever suspect she had help from someone in the hospital. Never. Girvin was the answer, I was sure of it. But I had to find out for certain, not that it would have made any difference.

I decided to ride my bike past Girvin's house at Fourteenth and Roosevelt and look for signs that she might be in the house---some lady's laundry drying on the clothesline in the backyard, perhaps, or a parted curtain in the front affording me a view of the living room. I wasn't sure what I would discover.

As I got near to the house, I barely recognized it as Girvin's. The yard was littered with scraps of paper and other debris. Unread newspapers were still on the porch, in exactly the same place where they were delivered. Girvin had evidently left town or had moved. It was certainly apparent that the house hadn't been lived in for several days. I didn't know what to think. My first thought was that he and Winnie Ruth had taken off and were living together somewhere, but I quickly realized the notion was preposterous. What could they possibly see in each other? How often does a guy need a haircut anyway? I decided that the whole affair wasn't any of my business, and I wheeled around and rode my bike home.

9

I READ AN ACCOUNT of Girvin's murder on page one of The Republic under a three column headline.

MALE NURSE FOUND SLAIN, POLICE HUNT SUSPECT

PHOENIX, March 21 The badly beaten body of a male nurse employed at the Arizona State Hospital was discovered early this morning in his home at 1412 Roosevelt Street. Police identified the body as that of Frank Girvin, 38, who resided at that address.

The slain man shared his home with another employee of the hospital who police identified as Neil Soderquist, 37. Authorities at the hospital told police that Soderquist had not reported for work in four days and had not notified them of his absence. He is presently being sought for questioning.

Girvin had been repeatedly beaten around the head with a heavy object, according to Police Lieutenant Fred P. Zeeman. An autopsy will be performed to determine the exact cause of death, he said.

The body was discovered by Bobby Gleason, 13, of 712 Sixth Street, a carrier for the Arizona Republic. Gleason had approached the home when he noticed that previously delivered newspapers were still on the doorstep. His suspicions led to the discovery of the body, Zeeman said.

Police said that Gleason will be cited for his good citizenship.

I dropped the newspaper and ran down the hall to Floyd's apartment. No one was home. I scribbled a note to Floyd and shoved it under the door: *Good news. Come to the drugstore as soon as you read this. I'll be there till six.*

Floyd showed up just as Norm was closing. "So what's the big news? Did you get laid or something?"

"Hold on a second. I'll walk with you."

We walked north on Third Street toward McDowell.

"Are you going to tell me why you brought me down here, or not?"

"Floyd, you won't believe this, but Girvin is dead. It's in this morning's paper, in black and white."

"Girvin, the queer? I don't believe it."

"It's true, so help me."

"Who did it?" Floyd asked.

"The paper said it was his roommate, but personally I think you did it."

"Hey, don't look at me," Floyd said. "It was the torpedoes I brought in from Brooklyn. Not me. I just did what you asked me to do. I'm clean. I'm no goddamn trigger man."

"Maybe not," I said, "but you're still an accessory."

"If you want to know the truth, Artie, I think you did it. I think you and the roommate were butt-fucking and I think Girvin caught you two in the act."

"That's swell, Floyd, really swell."

"The way I see it, there's this fight. Girvin goes after his roommate, fire in his eyes, and starts to choke him. You don't want anything to happen to the roommate 'cause he's a better butt-fucker, so you go after Girvin. In the meantime, the roommate goes into the bedroom and comes out with a gun. You try to wrestle the gun away from the roommate. There's a lot of pushing and shoving. The gun goes off. Girvin falls over dead. Suddenly you notice that you're holding the gun. You stand there bewildered, looking down at the pistol. Artie, do you remember how John Garfield looked in *They Made Me A Criminal* when they told him that he killed John Ridgely, the guy who played the reporter?

"Well," Floyd continued, "Garfield gets that dazed look on his face and he says, 'Wha? wha?'---Not what, what?---just 'wha?' That's how you looked, Artie, when you saw the gun in your hand. You couldn't believe it, could you? Anyway, the roommate looks down at Girvin's body, then he looks at you. 'I'm getting out of here,' the roommate says. 'Wait,' you say, 'aren't we going to continue where we left off?' He runs out the door and leaves you standing there, the gun in one hand, your johnson in the other."

"I hate to disappoint you, Floyd, but Girvin wasn't shot, he was hit over the head with a blunt instrument."

"Okay, so there was no gun, so you hit him over the head with your johnson."

"Jesus, Floyd, talking to you is impossible."

"Well, you may not have killed him but you can't deny you wanted to see him dead."

"To be honest, I did."

"Well, for your sake," Floyd said, "I hope the cops don't pick you up for questioning."

"Are you kidding me again?"

"No, I'm not, Artie."

"Then why would you bring something like that up? Why would you say that? About the cops, I mean."

"I don't mean that you'd be a suspect," Floyd said, "but they might want to know what you know about Girvin and his roommate."

"I never even saw his goddamn roommate."

"Well, they might want to ask you that anyway. They might want to know if you ever saw anything strange going on at the house, By the way, who found the body?"

"The paper boy," I said, "one of the guys who took my place."

"I'm not trying to scare you, Artie, but wouldn't it make sense for the cops to talk to some of the other paper boys?"

"I guess you're right."

"Don't worry about it. If they come to see you, just tell them the truth."

"Yeah," I said, trying not to look too concerned.

"You've got that John Garfield look on your face," Floyd said.

We reached the apartment building. "I'd better go now," I said. "My mother has dinner ready."

"I've got a date," Floyd said. "I'll see you later. Don't worry about the cops. They probably won't even show up. If they do, don't tell 'em you wanted to see the sonofabitch dead."

"Jesus," I said under my breath, "Oh, Jesus."

I felt sick to my stomach. Whatever relief I felt about Girvin's murder had disappeared. I felt implicated. I saw myself being hauled into the police station and grilled by a couple of burly cops. If the cops couldn't find Girvin's roommate, they might try to force a confession out of me. There were plenty of witnesses who saw Girvin taunting me in the drugstore. For sure they'd say I had a motive.

Dear Lord, I admit I wanted Girvin dead. I prayed for it to happen. But listen to me, God, I take it all back. Make him be alive, make him come back to earth. But I knew it was too late. If God had answered my prayers once, how could I expect God to change things back again. Answered prayers don't come with erasers on them.

I thought about the movie I saw at the Orpheum. It was called *Love Affair* and it starred Charles Boyer and Irene Dunne. There was song in it I remembered:

Wishing will make It so
Just keep on wishing and cares will go
Dreamers tell us dreams come true
That's no mistake.

I wanted the police to find the roommate and I wanted the roommate to confess, and then everything would be okay. That's what I wished, for then there wouldn't be any further investigation. But what if the roommate denied everything and told the police he got scared and ran away when he saw Girvin's body? It happens all the time. Guys panic and run away. Or worse, what if the police find the roommate dead somewhere? Either way, the investigation would continue, and sooner or later the cops would come after me. I couldn't stand thinking about it. I wondered if I shouldn't go to the police right away and confess. I would tell them very calmly that Girvin had been threatening me. No, that wouldn't be true. No, he hadn't threatened me, but he'd picked on me. Yes, he was picking on me, that was it. He was picking on me is what I'd tell the homicide detective.

"But you don't go around killing people just because they're picking on you," the detective would say.

"I didn't kill him, sir, I would say. "I only wished he were dead."

"It's the same thing," the detective would tell me. Then he would place his hand on my shoulder and in a fatherly way explain to me that sometimes wishing will make it so.

I needed someone to help me figure things out. I didn't want to talk to any policemen and I didn't want to go to the police station. I couldn't go to the rabbi---he'd only take Girvin's side. Besides, the rabbi would tell me that God answered my prayers just to teach me a lesson---that prayers shouldn't be used for spiteful and vindictive reasons: they should be used to benefit mankind, or better yet to help the Jews find a homeland in Palestine. Important things. Positive things. Not like asking him to rub out some meaningless creep from an insane asylum.

I imagined that, as the rabbi was explaining these things to me, his middle finger---the one he used to shove into Myron Newmark's rectum---was wiggling back and forth and up and around until I thought I'd surely become cross-eyed from watching it.

ARLENE GOT UP from the dinner table when I opened the door. She and Rex had already started eating.

"Where have you been, Arthur?" she said angrily. "It's almost 7:30. We had to start without you."

"I had to finish my deliveries." I said. I didn't like lying, but it seemed best under the circumstances. I wasn't in the mood for answering a lot of questions. Anyway, she couldn't be angry if she thought my reason for being late had to do with making extra money.

I shook hands with Rex.

"How are you, Arthur?" said Rex Alderdice.

"Pretty good," I replied.

Evidently my reply was so spiritless that Rex looked surprised. "Just pretty good?"

"Okay, I guess."

"Well, that's not much better, is it? In fact, Arthur, 'okay, I guess' sounds even worse that 'pretty good,' don't you think?"

"I guess you're right."

Arlene returned from the kitchen with a plate of food. "Look," she said, "I have your favorite---brisket and potato pancakes."

"I'm not very hungry," I said.

"What do you mean? It's brisket, your favorite. I made it for you."

"I don't feel like eating."

"Taste it," she said, "just taste it."

I took a couple of bites, then pushed the plate away. "If I eat any more I'll throw up," I said. "I think I'll go for a walk."

"But you just came home."

"I know. I won't be gone long."

"Arthur, is something the matter?"

"What makes you say that?"

"What makes me say that?" she said, repeating my question. "What makes me say that? He comes home looking like he lost his best friend. He doesn't eat his dinner. He's home five minutes and he wants to take a walk. What do you mean, 'what makes me say that'?"

"I'm tired, that's all."

"So go to bed early. Mr. Alderdice will be leaving soon."

I walked toward the door, "I'll be back in a little while. Goodnight, Mr. Alderdice." I waved to Rex, closed the door and walked through the corridor, down the building steps and out into the darkness of Central Avenue. I had a lot to think about.

I started walking south on Central Avenue toward the Westward Ho. I thought about Des Moines and how much I missed it. I missed Annabel Knobloch and how well she ironed the clothes my father sent me. I missed my Aunt Ida's house and her warm kitchen with the beef soaking in pans of salt water. I even missed my cousin Moose. Life then was comfortable, protected, serene. There was no Winnie Ruth Judd around to hound me. There was no Frank Girvin, no Marvin Hooks,

ON THAT EVENING in Phoenix, as I left our apartment, I would have caught the first train east. But we get wiser as we grow older. I didn't realize how fortunate I was. Phoenix, despite the creeps that had come into my life, represented freedom from the constrictions of living with relatives, a way to ride in the front-of-the-bus for the first time in my life. I did not have to account to anyone for my actions. Phoenix had its Winnie Ruth Judds and Frank Girvins, yes, but it also had its Myrna Handmachers and Floyd Antonellis and Katherine Antonellis.

On the other hand, Des Moines had its Old Jakes and Uncle Abes, a slew of straight-laced, small-minded relatives, and a life that could only be lived out in subservience. But I wasn't sharp enough back then, that night on Central Avenue, to realize it.

When I came back to the apartment later that evening, Rex and Arlene were on the balcony talking, unaware that I had returned. I undressed quietly and got into bed. Their voices carried into the living room.

"I've never seen him this way," I heard my mother say. "Do you think something's the matter?"

"Well, he does look a little worried," Rex said. "Something probably happened in school, is my guess. Kids his age get upset pretty easily."

"I wish you'd talk to him sometime."

"What would you like me to talk to him about?"

"Oh, I don't know, just anything to find out what's on his mind."

"You know I can't do that." I detected an edginess in Rex's voice.

As I listened to them, I felt like a cadaver on a mortuary slab, the mourners standing over me doing an autopsy of my brain. I wanted to tell them the real story---my worry about the police coming after me and my fear of Winnie Ruth. That would really give them something to talk about. If I did, they'd probably faint dead away on the spot.

My mother was arguing: "I don't see what's wrong with it."

Rex said, his voice rising slightly: "Arlene, we've gone over that a hundred times. I like Arthur. I like him very much, but I'm not his father. Try to understand."

"I'm not asking you to be his father," she snapped back. "I'm only asking you to talk to him. I can't do it, and there's no one else---no one. I have to be everything to him---mother, father, breadwinner. It's too much." She was crying.

"Now don't start that." I heard him sigh. "You and I are good friends, Arlene, more than that, but I can't get involved in your life. I have my own family. If I got involved in Arthur's life it would mean---"

"Mean what?" I heard the anger in her voice. "Finish what you were going to say."

"It would mean that Arthur would start thinking of me as his father. For God's sake, you know the rule we operate under."

"Stop talking like that," she said. "You're not in the office now."

"We have to be very careful. There's too much at stake."

"But you could at least talk to him...."

"You've got to realize that just because Arthur's father has shirked his responsibilities doesn't mean that Arthur suddenly has to become my responsibility. If you and I were married, which we're not, it would be a different matter. But I can't do Ben Randall's job for him, and I won't."

Their conversation was getting tiresome. I didn't want to hear any more. I rolled over on the bed and pulled the pillow over my ears.

10

FRANK GIRVIN HAD been dead for several weeks, and I continued to fear the arrival of the police. I scoured The Republic and The Gazette every day for news of the case. I waited for the cops to pull me out of class at PUHS. At home, I ran for the mailbox after school, just in case there should be a letter from the police station. I jumped at every knock on the front door and cowered when the telephone rang.

There was nothing. No police, no newspaper story, nothing at all. But I felt no relief, only a growing expectation of being implicated. I knew the police had files on unsolved crimes that could remain open for years, decades, even centuries. So even if I hadn't heard from the police by now, eventually they would find me. The suspense would never end. It was a life sentence, an imprisonment in a jailhouse of fear.

I thought of John Garfield in *Dust Be My Destiny*, Garfield walking along the railroad tracks, the collar of his dark suit turned up, his grey fedora tilted over his eyes and, now and then, furtive glances over his shoulder.

Garfield, my idol, always on the lam.

Somebody looking closely at me might notice a new timidity in the set of my jaw. I felt like I was shrinking into the ground---like the *pisher* I had been in Des Moines. Guilt and remorse were in my heart. Did I actually kill Girvin or did I merely wish him dead? Or, under some weird hypnotic spell, did I break into his house and hit him over the head with a fireplace poker? I was so mixed up, I couldn't be sure of anything.

In June, I would be a senior at PUHS. I continued working at the soda fountain and making deliveries. I did my work routinely, exhibiting the skills of an experienced soda jerk, handling even the most elaborate orders with speed and accuracy. Scarcely a day went by without my being given a pat on the back by Norm. Even Marvin Hooks had little to criticize. But none of it meant a thing to me.

Myrna Handmacher. How I loved her. She still dropped by the store for her chocolate sundaes twice---sometimes three times---a week, and she wouldn't let anyone else wait on her. Even if I was busy and Hooks or one of the girls was free, she insisted on waiting for me. Most of the time she leaned over the counter and kissed me. If she didn't kiss me, I felt like she didn't like me anymore, and I would brood about it for days. But on a following visit she would bestow a kiss on me, and I would curse myself for having been such a fool. And then I would become so filled with joy that I didn't care if I went to jail or not.

I didn't know what made me feel worse---my anguish over Girvin's murder or my unfulfilled desire for Myrna. I suffered either way. When I saw her I became so exhilarated I could have jumped over the soda fountain, but when she didn't show up I would be plunged into despair, missing the toss of her dark hair, her smile, that bright loving smile that tore out my heart, and her maddeningly tempting breasts---full, sloping and as smooth as a caress. I didn't care if the heat soared to 120-degrees or if a sandstorm buried me in the desert or if tarantulas swarmed over the city---I didn't care as long as I was with Myrna.

At night I had visions of her spreading her legs, her thighs soft and silky. I would pull out my enormous johnson, bigger even than Dagwood's in the eight-pagers. Myrna would lie there staring at it, her mouth gaping in wonder, begging for it but at the same time crying shamelessly over the ecstasy she was about to experience when I finally put it in.

I was so obsessed that I felt I would go crazy if I didn't have some contact with her. During those times I'd phone her home, hoping to hear her voice, and when she answered I would hang up abruptly, returning the receiver to its cradle with the urgency of someone who'd grabbed the wrong end of a hot poker---too afraid of engaging her in conversation outside of our usual meeting place.

One time, hoping to catch a glimpse of her, I hid behind a large palm tree in front of her house, but I was so afraid she might see me that I stayed there, hugging the rough bark of the tree until dark, until I could slink away in the night, unnoticed. I hated even thinking about the risks I took.

I was sixteen and had never had real sex. The closest I came was with Lila Borenstein. I first met her in Sunday school. I knew she liked me because she always wanted to hang around me. She stared at me continually with a sick-puppy look on her face. She was a dark, dumpy girl with a pretty face. If I hadn't already known her, she would be the kind of girl someone would try to fix me up with. We were both Jewish, she was short and so was I, and we were both seniors.

Once I found myself alone with her in the book stacks of the library. We were in the history section, researching papers on the Civil War. She was still wearing that sick-puppy expression, and since no one was around I mustered up the courage to kiss her. I expected her to slap my face, but instead she threw her arms around my neck and pushed herself against me. I put my hand under her blouse and then under her brassiere.

Right there in the school library, too. Jesus.

From then on we met frequently, sometimes at her home, sometimes in Encanto Park. I was never able to have intercourse with her, though. I tried to, but in a way I was glad she said no. When it came down to it, I was afraid and, besides, I really didn't want to do it with her anyway. I felt no passion for Lila, not the way I imagined I would with Myrna.

ONE AFTERNOON AS I reported for work, I saw Myrna seated at the counter. I checked with Norm. There were no deliveries to be made. I quickly put on my cap and apron and went behind the counter, barely able to hide my elation at seeing her. She was drinking a lemonade. It wasn't like her to be drinking lemonade.

"Hi, Myrna," I said. "No sundae?"

She looked up from the book she was reading. "Oh, Hi, Arturo. I don't know, I guess I didn't feel like a sundae, and besides, you weren't here to make it for me."

"Are you all right, Myrna?"

"I guess so," she said. "I'm sort of worried about exams, and there's so much else going on in my life. I have to be in the right frame of mind to enjoy a sundae."

"Can you tell me what's wrong?" I asked. "I mean, sometimes it helps to talk it out."

"Arturo, you're really my best friend, but it's a secret. It wouldn't be right to tell you, even though I know you wouldn't say anything."

"You can trust me, Myrna."

"If you only knew how many boys have said that to me."

"I don't understand what you mean."

"What I mean, Arturo, is that I can't rely on anything that boys tell me, and that's what's wrong with me, if you must know the truth."

"Myrna, what happened? Please tell me."

"Are you sure you want me to?"

"Yes, I'm sure, very sure."

She paused, then looked down at the counter. "Arturo, dear, I'm dropping out of State in May and going back to Kansas City. I won't be back for a while."

She called me "dear," and that was the first thing I heard. Then I felt my knees grow weak and my head begin to spin as the news sank in. *I love you, Myrna. I love you more than anything. Tell me you were just kidding. Look at me. Don't turn your head away. Why do you want to leave me? Oh, God, what have I done?*

"But... why, Myrna... why?" I pleaded, struggling to get the words out.

"Arturo, I'm so afraid you'll hate me. It's so hard to tell you---so hard, harder even than telling my parents. I know how you feel about me, and maybe if we were closer in age I'd feel differently about you. But there's another boy in my life. There has been for a long time."

"I know that."

"I saw you standing behind a tree in front of my house. I knew then how you felt about me. I knew then that you loved me. No boy would do that unless he loved me."

I wanted to go someplace and hide. I was filled with shame, and I hated myself. I was no better than a Peeping Tom, and now I was discovered by the girl I loved in the worst sort of deviant act. It was as if she had caught me with my hand in my trousers whacking off. *Myrna, oh, Myrna. Now I know I really love you. You are beautiful and kind and gentle. Anyone else would have called me a degenerate, but not you, Myrna. I will always love you, always and forever.*

"I'm sorry, Myrna. I do love you. I can't help it."

"I know, dearest, and that's why I have to tell you..."

"Tell me what?"

She took a deep breath and turned away from me as she spoke. "I'm going to have a baby, Arturo."

Everything before my eyes turned into a blur. I felt my heart hammering in my chest. I clutched at the counter with both hands. I knew what God was doing. God knew everything, and He was paying me back for the blackness in my heart, for putting my finger in Lila Borenstein's hole, and---God help me---for willing the death of Frank

Girvin. I was God's mistake, a filthy pariah with so many black marks next to my name in the Book of Life that there was no room left on the parchment.

I walked out from behind the counter and sat down next to her. She looked away from me. I placed my hand in hers.

"I love you, Myrna," I said. She spun around on her stool to face me, then she buried her head in my chest and began to cry.

"Don't cry, Myrna."

"Arturo, there's something else."

"Yes?"

"The father, Arturo, do you know who it is?"

"No, and I don't care anymore."

"He knows you, Arturo. He's your best friend. He's worried about you."

"Floyd? Floyd Antonelli?" I didn't believe it.

"Yes, Arturo, Floyd."

I sighed and let my head drop on the counter. I sat there saying nothing, feeling my heart pounding within my chest and inside my throat and reverberating within my skull until I thought the top of my head would explode.

I was dying. Oh, God, I was dying. There was nothing left. Help me, Lord, you who have an exact account of my sins, help me. Farewell, Myrna. Farewell, Floyd. Farewell to everything good in my life.

I tried to regain my composure. "What about the baby? I mean, what will happen to you, Myrna?"

She put her arm on my shoulder. "I don't know," she said. "Floyd wants to marry me, but we don't have any money right now, and Floyd just joined the Navy, so maybe in a year or so the baby and I will join him, wherever he is. It'll work out, Arturo."

"I didn't know he joined the Navy---the poor Navy. I haven't seen him in more than a month."

"I know you haven't. He's been doing construction work in Utah. He's waiting to be called. His mother doesn't know about the Navy, so don't say anything to her. And she certainly doesn't know he's gotten a girl in trouble."

She dried her eyes with a napkin, slid off the stool and kissed me goodbye. Oh, what a sweet kiss she gave me. I shall never forget it.

"I'll come in again before I go to Kansas City," she said, and headed for the door.

"Goodbye, Myrna," I called after her.

Ah, Myrna.

THE REST OF the day I thought about nothing but Myrna and Floyd. I couldn't be angry with Floyd. After all, he was my best friend. He couldn't have known how I felt about Myrna. Better Floyd than some jerk of a football player. I was thinking about them when I walked into the apartment to have dinner. Rex was there, reading The Gazette.

"Hi, Mr. Alderdice."

"Hello, Arthur, ready for baseball? Opening day tomorrow, you know."

"What?"

"Season opener tomorrow. Cubs and Giants."

"Oh, yeah, I forgot."

"Hubbell will definitely pitch for the Giants. Who do you think will start for the Cubs? Larry French or Bill Lee?"

"I dunno."

Rex folded The Gazette and laid it on the floor next to his chair. And then he said: "I thought you used to get pretty whipped up about baseball. You don't sound too interested anymore."

"I guess I'm not, anymore."

Arlene stood in the doorway of the kitchenette, listening. "Arthur, you're in one of your stupors again. I'm getting a little tired of the way you're acting."

"I can't help it," I replied. "There are some things on my mind."

"What things?" she asked.

"Oh, just things."

"What things?" she persisted, expecting me to come up with something nice and goofy---something she could understand. Like, I lost my algebra book, or I got a flat tire on my bike. Jesus, how I hated that question. Why couldn't she just put dinner on the table and keep quiet. What could she possibly know about Girvin's murder or about Myrna leaving me and about Floyd joining the Navy, about the crazy house and Winnie Ruth. About anything.

What things? Jesus.

"Arthur," Rex said, "your mother is concerned about you. When you're not happy she's not happy either."

"I guess I know that, Mr. Alderdice."

"Listen, Arthur, I don't want you to think I have all the answers about life. There's a lot I don't understand in spite of my advanced years. Life is damn puzzling, for all of us---you, me, everyone. But when you're sixteen, you're suddenly faced with dilemmas that you haven't had to face before, and they become strange and very formidable. Unfortunately, you don't have the experience to take them in stride. And neither did I, when I was your age. Experience is a very good teacher, Arthur. It helps us to adjust to adversity. Do you follow me?"

"Yes, sir."

"One more thing---I hope you don't mind my speaking freely..."

"No, sir."

"Well," said Rex, "most boys your age have fathers around while they're growing up, and they learn from their fathers. If they haven't experienced things in life, they learn by observing their fathers. I certainly did. My dad taught me to play baseball and football, and back in Cleveland, where I grew up, he took me to see the Indians play---I don't know---at least a dozen times a year. And the way I am today was largely learned from observing my father. I'm still an Indians fan. I can't help myself. It's in my blood just as it was in my father's blood. Unfortunately, you've had to make your own way without the guidance of a father, and that's very hard---very, very hard. I don't know how or why you became a Cubs fan. It's something you did on your own, just like all the other things you've done on your own. No father. No older brother. No one to help you frame your character as a man."

I listened intently, occasionally nodding.

"Now I grant you," Rex went on, "that not all fathers are worth imitating. It's too bad, but a lot of sons grow up under the influence of the wrong characters, and sometimes---if that's the case---a boy is far better off being like you, fashioning his own character rather than soaking up the father's bad habits. It's not that your own father wouldn't have been a good influence on you. It's just that---well, sometimes we have to play with the cards that life deals us. Do you understand?"

"I think so," I said.

"I want you know one more thing, Arthur. If you ever need a friend to talk things over with, I'll be here for you."

Rex looked at my mother. "It'll be between Arthur and me, Arlene. Do you understand that"

She nodded.

"And you, Arthur, do you understand? Just you and me."

"Yes."

While Rex spoke, I had listened carefully. I heard the words and understood exactly what he was saying, but at the same time, I couldn't help thinking that this hulk of a man was doing it with my mother. I liked Rex, but there was no way I could talk to him about all the things that were troubling me. Every evil thought, every sinful action, all those rotten secrets would lay buried in my heart forever.

I got up from the dinner table and cleared the dishes. Then I headed for the front door.

"Where are you going, Arthur?"

"Out for a walk."

"Haven't I taught you to say 'excuse me' when you leave the table?"

"I forgot."

"Aren't you going to thank Mr. Alderdice?"

"Thank you," I said.

"That's okay, Arthur."

"I forgot to mention it, Arthur," she added, "but can you get off work at five, instead six, next Saturday? The Krakauers have invited us for a swim and dinner. They would also like you to stay overnight. Her kids are crazy about you. Of course, you know that. You can leave after breakfast Sunday, unless you want to stay longer and swim."

"Oh, Jesus," I said. "I don't want to go. Absolutely not."

"Don't tell me 'no.' You have to go, and that's all there is to it." There was a firmness in my mother's voice that I hadn't expected.

"Why do I have to go? Just give me one reason."

"I'm not going to get into a discussion with you," she said. "You're going, and that's final. If you had any idea how many nice things the Krakauers have done for us. We didn't know a soul when we came to Phoenix. Dorothy took us under her wing. You and I owe her plenty, Arthur. When she makes a point of asking you to stay over with Kyle, that's little enough repayment. I just don't understand you."

"She's a bitch, a nosey bitch."

"'What did you say?" she shouted.

"Nothing."

"You're not ever to use that kind of language again. Do you understand? Oh, God, now I'm upset." She continued her shouting. "Why do you do this to me? Have you no feeling for me? Don't you know what I've gone through all my life?"

I looked over at Rex. He had resumed reading the Gazette and appeared not be aware of the conversation.

"Okay, I'll go," I said. I couldn't listen to her anymore. I opened the door and walked out. I glanced at the door of Katherine Antonelli's apartment, wishing she was there, wishing Floyd was there.

11

I GOT INTO BED at the Krakauers with my algebra book shortly after ten. My room was just off the patio where I usually slept when I stayed overnight. I would have been happier if I had something more entertaining to read, but exams were coming up soon, and algebra was my weakest subject. After struggling to stay awake, I decided it would be futile to read any further, and shortly before eleven I switched off the light.

Immediately, I thought about Myrna, imagining that I was sleeping next to her. Thinking about her was always comforting. Somehow it was even more appealing thinking about her with a baby inside her stomach. I had often wondered if girls were hotter when they were pregnant; I was sixteen and didn't know about things like that. I didn't even know how semen was manufactured or where in a girl's vagina it had to be targeted in order to make a baby, or whether it was some kind of a sin to waste my semen as I had done so often without any intended destination for it.

One time, in Lila Borenstein's living room, she made me use a rubber while we were fooling around because she didn't want any sticky stuff on her mother's davenport. I didn't mind that so much, but after it was over she carefully removed the rubber, tied a knot in the end of it, and was about to stick the rubber, semen and all, in the side pocket of her dress. What the hell for? I wanted to know. She explained to me that she didn't trust me not to toss it someplace where her parents might find it. What riled me up was that she hadn't given me enough credit to dispose of my own rubber in a trash can. It occurred to me that someday she might want to inject herself with my semen and get herself knocked up and then bring a paternity suit against me, like Elaine Barry did with Charlie Chaplin. I remember trying to take the rubber away from her, but she wouldn't give it up, and there we were on her parents' davenport playing tug-o-war with the rubber. The next day I asked Floyd how long semen could keep before it lost its potency, but he just shook his head and called me a fucking idiot.

I was about to fall asleep when I heard a light knock at the door. The door opened before I could respond.

"Arthur, are you still awake?" It was Dorothy Krakauer. She spoke in a stage whisper. "I have to get a few things out of the closet."

"I'm awake," I said. "I turned out the light only a second ago."

She opened the closet door, turned on the closet light and took out a bathrobe and nightgown. She walked to the side of my bed.

"I'm forever forgetting things," she said. "Sometimes I wonder where my head is. By the way, Arthur, did you enjoy your dinner and the swim? You're so quiet most of the time---I don't know whether you like coming here, or not."

"Oh, I like it fine, Mrs. Krakauer."

"Remember what I told you before---you're to call me Dorothy."

"Okay, Dorothy," I said.

"Good. Well, now that that's settled, tell me how you're getting along in school?"

It was a goofy question to ask at eleven at night.

"School's fine," I said. "I'll be graduating this June."

"Hmm, I can hardly believe time has passed so quickly. You're quite grown up now, and a fine young man. I want Kyle to be just like you."

She glanced at my algebra textbook on the bedside table.

"I hated that subject with a passion."

"However," she went on, "I prefer to use the word 'passion' more constructively---say, in connection with love rather than hate, don't you agree?"

"Yes, Dorothy."

Something was happening. I couldn't figure it out. Why was she here? Why was she talking to me at this crazy hour---and talking in that nice, easy way as if we were the same age, not using her usual haughty tone? I watched her face, softer and more appealing now, her sharp nose and curly hair looking youthful in the soft glow of the closet light. I could tell she wanted to linger.

I was right.

"May I sit on your bed for a moment and talk?"

"Sure, Dorothy."

"Keep in mind that you and I are friends, and that anything we talk about is just between us. Fair?"

"I guess so, but what did you want to talk about?"

"Nothing important, really. I just want to know more about you. After all, you and Kyle are best friends. Right?"

Wrong. Floyd was my best friend, even if he had been screwing Myrna and had knocked her up.

"Right, Arthur?"

"I guess so," I lied.

"By the way, your mother went home after you went to bed. She said you could stay here as long as you wished."

"I'd better leave in the morning," I replied. "I have to get ready for finals."

"Well, school comes first," she said, "but you're welcome to stay the day if you wish."

"Thanks, Dorothy."

"Have you thought about college, Arthur?"

"Yes, a lot."

"Any school in particular?

"Oh, I dunno, Arizona U. Or State, either one. I'm not sure."

Abruptly, she took my hand. I couldn't be sure of her. What did she want? Was I only imagining that she was hot for it, or was it really so? I was confused. I kept my eyes fixed on her. She glanced over toward the bedroom door as if to make sure it was shut. Her teeth had closed over her bottom lip, her free hand covered mine and now she was moving it up and down my forearm in a steady motion, as though she had confused my arm with my johnson. I felt my body warming; my legs began to tremble. Finally, she spoke.

"Arthur, you're a wonderful young man. I hope Kyle will be just like you in every way. You're smart and kind and well-mannered." Her words were coming in a rush. "You're getting to be so big, too, and to think you're an only child with no father around."

Suddenly, she bent over and kissed my forehead, letting her lips slide down the side of my face. Then, while she was rubbing me she unleashed a barrage of questions, all delivered in a seductive tone. Things like: Is your mother having a good time in Phoenix? Does she have a man friend? Was she terribly unhappy with your father? All that stuff.

Meanwhile, with each question, the rubbing became more pronounced while I, best I could, tried to restrain myself from ejaculating. I would tell her anything, anything, if only she wouldn't stop. I could hear the voice of Leo Gorcey, telling me not to "*rat on me own mudder.*" I rose up from my bed and grabbed her pointed breasts and put my hands under her blouse.

What happened next is too terrible to think about. She suddenly stood up, her jaw tight, and in measured syllables, spoken in short bursts, said: "You ungrateful little slob! What in the name of hell do you think you're doing? I want you out of my house first thing in the morning. After all the things we've done for you and your mother." She grabbed the things she took from the closet and left the room, slamming the door shut on her way out.

I lay there shaking. I tried to reconstruct everything that happened---the way she kept rubbing me and kissing me. Nothing made any sense. Was I not supposed to respond to her? Rex would have the answer. He asked me talk to him when I needed help. Or maybe Katherine would have the answer. I didn't know where to turn.

I left the Krakauers early the next morning. No one was awake. I didn't want to see anyone.

12

THE POLICE PICKED up Neil Soderquist, Frank Girvin's roommate, two days before my graduation. He had been working at a tavern in Kingman, Arizona, and immediately confessed to Girvin's murder. I let out a big sigh of relief. There was nothing further to worry about with police. The Girvin chapter was closed. I couldn't have asked for a better graduation present. My only other concern was Winnie Ruth Judd. Her name was no longer on the pages of the newspaper, and it was if she had dropped off the edge of the world.

My Mother and Rex both came to my graduation, but did not sit together. It was fortunate that they didn't because the Krakauer family showed up---Dorothy, Kyle and Elizabeth. I must say, I was glad to see them. Dorothy, seemingly, was no longer angry with me, and in fact had slipped me an envelope with twenty-five dollars in it, at the same time extending her cheek for me to kiss. I had known that nothing would come of that weird night at her home because a few weeks later she invited Arlene and me for one of her picnic-swims. I had put up a fuss about going but as usual lost that battle.

I was worried about what Dorothy would do when she saw me. Would she treat me as an unbalanced child to be ignored? That was something I couldn't have dealt with. Or even worse, would she have said something to Arlene about my being a degenerate?

Whatever she might say, she would be discreet about it, I knew that much. Most likely, she'd say something like: "You might want to ask Arthur to tell you about what happened the night he slept over"---and that would have been damage enough. But nothing out of the ordinary took place. Dorothy was sweet and cordial and treated me with kindness, apparently afraid I would accuse her, in turn, of starting the whole mess.

I had a chance at my graduation to take stock of how little social progress I had made in Phoenix. I felt as if I had never left Alicia Baldwin's class that first day at Kenilworth school. I was still an outcast, the son of a transplanted "lunger." I had a nodding acquaintance with most of the students in my class, but there was none with whom I was interested in sharing pleasantries after the ceremony---and none, I'm sure, who really wanted to be seen talking with me. Lila Borenstein was an exception. She hung around me after the ceremony, looking very pretty in her white dress. I introduced her to my mother and Rex.

After the ceremony the three of us walked home, Rex, my mother and me. The heat was blistering. It was a long walk. We headed west on Seventh Street, then turned north on Central, passing Gross's Delicatessen. I wanted to stop for a corned beef sandwich, but Arlene said it would spoil my dinner, which she had made special for me in honor of my graduation. Besides, she had some really good news to tell me, which she said she'd like to deliver over dinner.

I could tell Rex would have liked to stop at Gross's. The heat was getting to him. He hadn't taken off his jacket, and the perspiration was beginning to show through his Palm Beach suit and around the rim of his white collar.

After dinner, Arlene gave me the news. Rex was being transferred to Chicago as head of the Bureau of Public Debt for the Midwest region, and he was taking my mother with him as his administrative assistant. Rex added that it would be a major promotion for my mother.

She didn't ask me what I thought of the idea. I sat there in silence, trying to figure out what it would mean. I probably would not see Myrna again unless she came back to Phoenix for a visit with Floyd. I had no place in either of their lives anymore and, besides, it would be hard being around them, feeling as I did about Myrna. I would miss the drugstore and Lila and Katherine Antonelli, and all the good things about Phoenix.

A FEW DAYS later, while I was trying to digest the news about leaving Phoenix, I heard about the death of Floyd Antonelli. He had been not just my best friend in Phoenix but actually the best friend I'd ever had. It was the first time that a real tragedy had struck my life. Not even my father's death had affected me as deeply. Floyd had been killed while serving on a destroyer in the South Pacific. I read his obituary in The Republic over and over, hoping that the print on the paper would suddenly change before my eyes. I didn't know what to do or who to turn to. I ran down the hall to Katherine's apartment, but she wasn't home. I was in a panic as I rode my bike down to the Adams Hotel restaurant where she worked. She wasn't there, nor did I expect her to be. I approached one of the waitresses, a tall woman with pockmarks on her face, her blond hair piled on top of her head like a bird's nest.

"Excuse me," I said, "I wonder if you could---"

"Hold on, Sonny, be with you in a minute." She gathered up some dirty dishes and placed them on a tray.

"Wuddya want?" she said, walking toward me.

"Have you seen Katherine Antonelli?" I asked.

"Nope."

"Well, do you know where I can find her?"

"I'm sure I wouldn't know," she replied.

"Do you know who would?"

"Maybe the manager, but he's not here now."

I thanked her and walked out. I had no idea where to go or who turn to, but I had to talk to someone about Floyd, someone who knew him and could recall stories about him---anything that might help bring him back to life for me, if only for a few short moments. I wanted to get in touch with Myrna, but I had no idea where to reach her or what to say to her if I did.

That evening I told Arlene about Floyd. She was saddened by the news. "I'll go down the hall and pay a call on Katherine," she said.

"You won't find her home."

"How do you know?"

"I tried."

"Poor Katherine. Poor Floyd. I really didn't know him well. I know you did, Arthur," she said.

"Yeah, I knew him real well." And then I felt the tears running down my cheeks. It was the first time I had cried in front of my mother, I suppose, since I was a baby.

I finally saw Katherine a few days later. Almost as an afterthought, I knocked on her door on my way to the drugstore, not really expecting to find her in. It caught me by surprise when she opened the door. I could tell that she had been drinking, and her eyes were swollen and red. When she saw me she emitted a slight sob, then threw her arms around me and commenced crying.

"Oh, Arthur, Arthur. Oh, Arthur."

She held me so tight I could scarcely breathe. I kissed her all over, her eyes, her face, her hair. We were both crying.

She drew her head back. "What am I going to do?" she asked, her eyes pleading. "I have no one now, only you. You were Floyd's best friend. Hold me tight, Arthur."

I held her so tight I could feel the press of her belly, the roundness of her breasts. I was overwhelmed with sympathy and longing. Shamefaced that I wanted her so badly at that moment of her grief, I abruptly pulled away from her. She re-positioned herself immediately so that our bodies were touching again, and I knew then that I could have taken to her bed if I chose to.

And Lord knows, I chose to, but too many thoughts were swimming around in my brain. For one thing, Floyd had been dead for only a few weeks, and I couldn't defile his memory by having sex with his mother. For another, she was so grief-stricken, so terribly vulnerable, that it would have been taking unfair advantage of her under such circumstances. At the time, I doubt whether I was rational enough to rattle off all the reasons why I couldn't do it with her, but I knew it would be wrong. Twice now I had rejected Katherine, all for seemingly plausible reasons, yet somewhere beneath the surface was one major reason that loomed larger than any other---and I had no clear idea of what it was.

JULY, 1942. THE wars in the Pacific and in Europe were heating up. I registered for the draft, but it seemed inconceivable that I would ever have to serve. My view of myself was as a scrawny kid whose courage, both moral and physical, had never really been put to the test, and if it were, I was sure I would fail. If I were to count the people in my life of whom I was afraid, the list would be endless---starting with my uncles in Des Moines and continuing on to Winnie Ruth Judd, Frank Girvin, Marvin Hooks, Dorothy Krakauer and Rabbi Cohen. Furthermore, if I were to be drafted, the list would go on to include both the German and Japanese armed forces, and maybe even our own.

My mother, in the meantime, had set a date for our departure to Chicago. I rode my bike to the drugstore and said goodbye to Norm. I think he was genuinely sorry to see me leave.

"What the hell do you want to go to Chicago for? That's a rough town, kid. Better wear your bullet-proof vest."

"Aw, it won't be so bad," I said, "and besides, I guess I won't be there too long. I'll probably be drafted soon."

"No kidding."

"I had to register the other day."

"As I said, kid, wear your bullet proof vest."

We shook hands.

"Let me know if you ever need a reference, Arthur. You did a good job."

"Thanks, Norm."

I walked behind the counter and said goodbye to Hooks. I may have been imagining it, but I think he was sad to see me leave. He put a scrawny arm on my shoulder, and then he said. "Watch your step, sheeny."

I DIDN'T RELISH saying goodbye to Lila. She was a good girl. I would miss her. When I rang her bell, she came charging out of her front door, a big smile on her face.

"Hi, Artie," she said. "This is an unexpected pleasure." She was wearing shorts and a flimsy blouse, and she looked very appealing in spite of her flabby thighs.

"Got a minute, Lila? There's something I want to talk to you about."

"Of course." She brought her lips to mine and kissed me, her mouth open wide.

"Are your parents home?" I asked.

"My father's at the store. I don't know where mom is. Come on in."

We walked into her living room and sat down.

I put my arm around her. "What I wanted to say, Lila..."

"Yes?"

"I have to leave Phoenix."

"You what?"

"I'm leaving Phoenix. My mother is being transferred to Chicago."

She said nothing, but sat quietly, staring at me.

"I can't believe what you're telling me, Arthur. I don't believe it."

"It's true, Lila. I'm sorry."

She turned her head away, and softly began crying. "I love you, Arthur," she whispered. "Do you have to go?"

"One way or the other, I'd have to. I'm going to be drafted pretty soon, probably when I'm in Chicago. I heard the army gives you a furlough after you finish basic training. If it's true, Lila, I'll come to see you when I'm on furlough. Anyway, I'll write to you"

"Promise me?"

"I promise."

I held her in my arms and kissed her. "I'll always love you," she said. Ah, Lila.

THE PROSPECT OF military service hovered over my head like a threatening cloud. It was hard to imagine what it would be like for me. Would I be killed in action like Floyd had been, or would I return blinded and lame, unable to take care of myself? I had no idea of what lay beyond that threatening cloud. Even if I should return in one piece, I wondered what the rest of my life would be like. I was a good student at PUHS, but not a distinguished one, and I sensed that I couldn't get into a good school on an academic scholarship. Furthermore, I was without any special gifts and, more importantly, had no desire to do anything in particular with my life except get away from my mother and bury my head in the ample bosoms of Myrna (wherever she was) and Katherine Antonelli.

I had two pieces of unfinished business to take care of before I left Phoenix. One was to say goodbye to Katherine and reassure her that I would be back as soon as I could. It would turn out, however, to be a more painful farewell than I had imagined because when I told her that my mother and I were leaving Phoenix, she immediately put her arms around me and burst into tears, pleading hysterically for me not to go. Since I was so closely connected to Floyd, it was as if my departure, in her mind, would represent the ultimate death of Floyd. I suspected that If I had chosen to have sex with her, it would not be Arthur Randall taking her to bed, but (as I would later come to realize with certainty) a fusion of two young men performing the act---one living, one dead.

My final mission was to confront my fear of Winnie Ruth Judd head-on, for I had read somewhere that by doing so, the fears would eventually resolve themselves. And that is why I rode my bike over to the Arizona State Hospital late one afternoon on that scorching July day.

13

I RODE EAST ON Van Buren until I reached Twenty-Second Street, then turned north a block until I reached the back of the hospital's grounds. From where I stood, I could see the inmates on the grounds: the epileptics, the hopelessly retarded, the demented and the criminally insane. It was a horrible spectacle, and I wondered where I had found the courage to be there. Winnie Ruth would not be among them, for she had escaped late in 1939 and had been in and out of the hospital ever since. It would be best if I could stare Medusa in the face, but barring that I could try to imagine that I was in Winnie Ruth's shoes, standing near to where she had once stood, and through her eyes be able to see the other inmates shuffling about in the sun, just as she had seen them.

I had seen several pictures of her in The Republic, one in particular when she was apprehended in which her mouth was turned down in a pout; her hand revealed a bandage over a wound she had sustained while dismembering her victims. But the one I remembered most vividly showed her in a torn hospital gown, her bare shoulder, slender and delicate, raised so that a small growth of hair was revealed from under her armpit. It was a photograph I shall always treasure. It seemed highly unlikely that such a rare flower, even one so violent, could have existed among these inmates.

Even as a young boy in Des Moines, I had played the same game of pretending in connection with my father--- as I had with Winnie Ruth---imagining that I was his shadow, walking where he had walked, seeing the things he had seen. At best, my father himself was a shadowy figure to me, for I had never seen him face to face except as a toddler. I had a few of his pictures to fuel my imagination, one of him and Arlene taken on their honeymoon at Pikes Peak (she once told me that she was terrified of being in the mountains, but I have since concluded that my father's presence and the prospect of losing her innocence there were more terrifying to her than the mountains themselves). There was a photograph of him in his army uniform (he was a corporal) taken at Camp Dodge, Iowa, in 1919. Nor for that matter had I ever seen Winnie Ruth face-to-face; like my father, she was alive only through her photographs.

Those many years, after I was discharged from the army, I was still playing the same game in connection with my father. I had visited an army buddy, Captain John Behl, at his home in Tulsa. He was a good friend who was to die a few years later, and after we said goodbye I walked around downtown Tulsa looking for the site of the old Mayo Hotel. I knew nothing about the town or the hotel other than that Tulsa was one of my father's ports-of-sales-calls, along with the Broadview Hotel in Wichita, the President in Kansas City, and the Brevoort in Chicago. I had received letters from him from all these cities and always on stationery from the same hotels. The letters were written in a large scrawl in black ink and signed "Your loving father." I can't remember a word he wrote; I was concentrating instead on those magic words--- *Your loving father*---for the words were concrete proof that he still liked me, even though he never came around to tell me so. The letters came from far off places, and I would stare in wonderment at the overly-glamorized line-drawings of the outside of the hotels. The Mayo itself gave rise to my most romantic instincts, for wasn't Mayo the first name of Humphrey Bogart's wife, Mayo Methot, who was an actress and perhaps might even have known my hero, John Garfield?

Standing in front of the hotel I see beyond the shuttered exterior into the building's ornate lobby of long ago, where fat-cat oilmen wearing cowboy boots sit around in upholstered chairs, each chair within spitting distance of a polished spittoon atop a rubber mat. Clusters of beautiful women, fashionably attired, stand in small groups talking, their eyes taking in the swaggering oilmen in the lobby.

I see my father walking toward the desk clerk, a diminutive man wearing a brown suit and a brown fedora. He glances boldly at the beautiful women. He speaks to the desk clerk. "Any messages for me?"

"Just one, Mr. Randall," the clerk replies, handing my father a slip of paper.

My father thanks the clerk, reads the message and shoves the paper in his pocket. *Game tonight, 7 sharp, at Izzy Berliner's store. Come to the back.*

I watch as my father gets into the elevator and heads for his room. As soon as he opens the door, he removes his coat and throws it on the bed. In the bathroom he washes, slaps after shave on his face and applies talc to help hide his beard. Now he walks over to his Gladstone and removes a clean shirt. After tying his tie, he puts his jacket back on, counts his cash and takes a last look in the mirror before heading for the lobby. He'll have to be careful with his cash, he reminds himself. A few winning hands early in the game and he'll be able to stick around and make a night of it. Otherwise, it'll be a glum evening alone in his hotel room.

Before leaving the hotel he stops at the coffee shop in the lobby and has a sandwich and coffee, then walks over to Cheyenne Street and Berliner's Jewelry Store. The store is dark except for a ribbon of light from the back room. He knocks on the front door. Presently, a short man in shirtsleeves appears. He and my father greet each other and together walk through the store into the back.

Three men are already seated around the table. They wave to my father, who pulls up a chair.

"Deal," says one man to Izzy, not wasting any time.

"Ante half-a-rock," says Izzy, dealing out five cards.

My father looks over his cards, discards two, then bets his new hand, which turns out to be a loser. More hands are dealt, more are lost. It's obvious that he's in the middle of a losing streak, which was not his plan. The game drones on. So far, Izzy is a big winner. My father wins one pot, then another, both small, but his winning hands are few and far between and his stack of chips is dwindling. He looks worried, and in order to recoup some of his losses starts betting wildly. "Let's get out of here," I want to tell him, but even if he could hear me there'd be no stopping him.

The game has gone on for two hours. Izzy is still the big winner, my father still the big loser. He's out of chips and dead broke. He has to leave. Izzy follows him out of the room and into the store.

"Not your night, eh, Ben."

"Guess not," my father replies.

"You'll get even next time," Izzy assures him.

"Izzy, I wonder..."

"What do you need, Ben?"

"Maybe if you could spare *fufsten tollar* for a few weeks?" (Many Jews spoke Yiddish when talking about money, apparently for fear of being overheard by gentiles.)

"Look here, Ben, you already owe me *funf und dreisik* from the last time."

"You'll get it, you'll get it."

"*Ah solchn veh*" (in a pig's ass)."

"No really," says my father, "you'll get it."

"Okay," says Izzy, "here's *tsen*, it's all I can spare."

My father looks down at the bill, crumples it in his pocket, and walks dejectedly down Cheyenne Street toward the hotel. There's barely enough money to pay his hotel bill, have breakfast and get back to Wichita.

I walk along beside him, watching his slumping shoulders, his slow agitated steps.

Oh, my father, my father.

14

ARLENE, AT THE last minute, decided to visit Des Moines for a few months before we settled in Chicago. It was not a wise decision because even before we arrived, the news of my mother's relationship with Rex Alderdice had reached her family. The stoolpigeon, of course, was Dorothy Krakauer, whose friendship with a Des Moines woman was responsible for my mother's introduction to the Krakauer family. I could have predicted it.

My mother had made arrangements for us to stay with her sister and brother-in-law, Bernice and Al Sussman. They lived on Kingman Boulevard on the west side of town. If she had known what a chilly reception was waiting for her there, she would have gone straight to Chicago. I wasn't privy to everything Bernice and Al said to her, but I could tell that harsh words were exchanged. I got the sense that my mother wasn't backing down, even though she had a lot of pressure on her. She was beholden to too many people, mainly to her brothers and sisters, who had lent her the money to go to Phoenix, but best I could tell, she stood her ground.

I discovered for the first time that she had an intense dislike for her relatives, with their small-town, small-minded ways, and it was no surprise that she wanted to get out of Des Moines and live her own life. If there was ever a case to be made against poverty, Arlene's was a prime example. I also discovered she was not truly the dependent soul that I had first believed her to be in Des Moines; instead, it was dependence borne entirely out of necessity. Once poverty had its grip on her, she was unable to regain her independence---the independence that had once enabled her to marry my father. As I saw things, she regained her independence in Phoenix after she met Rex Alderdice, but lost it again when their friendship ended, sometime around 1950. But such are the roller-coaster rides of the human condition.

Changes had taken place in Aunt Ida and Uncle Louis's household that prevented our return. Two of their daughters had married, each bringing her husband into the house. I don't believe Arlene and I could have squeezed in, although my aunt would somehow have tried to arrange accommodations. I was looking forward to a visit to Annabel Knobloch's dildo at Aunt Ida's, but alas, to my disappointment, she had left my aunt's employ and taken her dildo with her.

MY UNCLE AL was a burly, mercurial man who operated a consumer finance business in downtown Des Moines. He was only nominally in charge; Aunt Bernice made most of the important decisions. His only business function seemed to be placing harassing calls to customers who were behind in their loan payments--- "deadbeats," he called them, or "rat bastards" when they were significantly in arrears and their collateral (usually automobiles) had to be repossessed. He played handball four or five times a week at the YMCA, after which he would steam and shower, splash his face with Lilac Vegetal, and emerge from the "Y" depleted and irritable, looking like a lobster that had just been removed from a kettle of boiling water.

His other and by far his major occupation was *davening* (praying), which he performed every day after his breakfast. He would put on his *teffilin* (phylacteries) and commence rocking back and forth, chanting the Hebrew prayers in a droning monotone. If someone entered the room, he would speak to them, even carry on a conversation, while his praying, uninterrupted, droned on without missing a beat.

Uncle Al was Moose's father, and I don't think he was especially proud of Moose's athletic accomplishments. His fatherly duties were more concerned with getting his son to <u>daven</u> every morning.

Aunt Bernice had been my mother's severest critic when my mother married my father, and now---with the news that Arlene had a boyfriend, a gentile who had a wife and children---the atmosphere in the Sussman household was strained, even cold, not just toward my mother but to me as well. How does it go? "The sins of the mother..."

BERNICE, EVER THE loyal wife, had resigned herself to living with Al. Theirs was a bad marriage, probably even worse than my mother's. But Jews back then didn't get divorced---better to tough it out than suffer the disgrace of a failed marriage; true in most cases, except in my mother's. A guilt-ridden man, my Uncle Al read girlie magazines on the sly and then hid them in a drawer behind his easy chair in the living room, out of the reach of Moose. He had suffered from eczema ever since I can remember. It was the curse of his life. It appeared on the palms of his hands in angry blotches and caused him to sob out in anguish from the itching. I overheard stories that he had an inexhaustible sexual appetite, his wife being the recipient of his ardor. She raised five children in addition to managing the household and running the finance office. Hers was an early death from a cerebral hemorrhage brought on, I'm sure, by the infantile demands of her husband.

Meanwhile, Rex had settled in Chicago, and one fateful day, while he was inspecting some of the Midwest regional offices that fell under his jurisdiction, he stopped off in Des Moines. He checked into the Fort Des Moines hotel. Arlene met him there and ended up staying the night. That same night, Moose and I cruised around Des Moines looking for pickups. (The details of that evening remain imbedded in my memory.) We found two girls who had left their farm communities and come to Des Moines to work for Bankers Life. We drove out to the Tromar Ballroom, where the singer Tony Martin was fronting an orchestra. The admission tickets were too expensive, and we decided to drive to Fox's Ice Cream store for cones, the girls disappointed and petulant. My girl, a husky blond named Loretta, nevertheless let me cop a feel in the back seat, but that was all. We dropped them off at their apartment and drove home to Kingman Boulevard. As soon as we arrived, I heard the voice of my Uncle *Al*, shouting down from his bedroom window.

"Arthur, you're a bad influence on my family, and so is your mother. Both of you can stay the night, but in the morning pack your things and get out of here."

I heard the words but was strangely unmoved by them. All that I could think of was that sooner or later it had to happen.

15

THE FOLLOWING MORNING, Arlene and I moved into a rooming house at Thirty-seventh and Ingersoll. Aunt Bernice implored my mother to stay, but she wanted no part of the Sussman household, and within ten days we were on the train to Chicago. Rex had found us a one room apartment at Granville and Winthrop on the north side, and a week later I was at my draft board, asking to be called up. I wanted no part of living with Arlene in cramped surroundings. I'd had enough of one-room apartments and in-a-door beds

It is often said that soldiers who readily adjust to the regimen of military life "had found a home in the army." And so it was with me. Army barracks, pyramidal tents, pup tents and sleeping bags were more to my liking than living in cramped quarters with Arlene. I had mixed feelings about leaving her, for her various illnesses and complaints to me had become more frequent with my impending departure. I did feel guilty about leaving her alone (as if it were an obligation of my birth to take care of her), but with Rex in the picture I felt I could leave with a clear conscience.

I passed my army physical and waited to be called. Finally, in January, 1943, after a week at the induction center at Camp Grant, Illinois, I was shipped off to Camp Callan, California, for basic training. I messed up my basic training pretty badly, but was nonetheless deemed fit for service and received a ten-day furlough as a reward for my ineptitude.

True to my promise to Lila and Katherine, I took a train to Phoenix before returning home to visit Arlene. When I saw Lila, I knew I could go all the way with her, but had I done so it would have been pushing it, and I didn't want to be obligated for a debt I couldn't pay off. After I said goodbye to Lila and promised to do a better job of corresponding, I went back to our old apartment building and knocked on Katherine's door. She was slow to answer, but when she finally opened the door, she greeted me with a stunned silence. When my presence had finally sunk in, she let out a gasp and threw her arms around me. And then she began to cry.

"Arthur, Arthur," she cried, "it's you, it's really you. You look so handsome in your uniform. Oh, Arthur, my love, come in. Let me look at you."

I kissed her on the lips, and held her close. I knew then that it was Arthur Randall she was kissing, not Floyd. I let my hands slide under her nightgown, then over her breasts, her storied breasts. "Oh, Katherine," I breathed.

"Come here, Arthur." She grabbed my hands and led me over to her bed, and helped me off with my clothes: my wool uniform, my shirt. I kicked out my shorts and fell into bed with her. It was my first time. I felt no remorse about screwing Floyd's mother. I didn't care anymore. I wanted her so bad.

She called the restaurant and said she was sick and wouldn't be coming in.

We spent the rest of the day and that night in bed together, breaking only to go next door to Grosso's for dinner. She had a couple of bottles of wine in her closet, and later that evening we polished them off.

I left Phoenix the following morning for Chicago and never returned until after the war. I wept silently throughout Europe at the thought of Katherine and the time we'd spent together.

During the next few years I fought in five campaigns in Europe as an artillery observer with the 124th Gun Battalion, participating in the

Second Battle of Britain, in Normandy, and in the Battle of the Bulge, along with two additional campaigns in Germany. I bring this out to illustrate the changes that took place in the terror-stricken, guilt-ridden kid I was in Phoenix. Combat against the Germans during the cold winter of 1944-45 did more to dispel my unrealistic fears than any battery of behavioral scientists could have accomplished---that along with the closeness I felt for my fellow artillerymen, all of them my brothers.

As I said before, some men find a home in the army, and I was one of them. The army, in short, was my resurrection, my redemption.

I hardly gave a second thought to Winnie Ruth Judd during my years in the army, and in the years beyond. Oh, yes, there were tinges of fear that would erupt along the line, but all I had to do to dispel them was think about the more violent things that could occur. And what was an even more effective way of dealing with her was my eventual realization that Winnie Ruth Judd was merely a symbol, in encapsulated form, of all my other fears.

Winnie Ruth is dead, but there are too many questions remaining about her guilt or innocence to say that the case is closed. She denied that she had hacked up the bodies of her roommates, but not that she had murdered them. The surgical skills necessary to dismember the bodies point in some other direction. Some believe that Jack Halloran hired someone to do the deed, but that was never brought out as part of the evidence. In any case, Winnie Ruth, despite all my fears, was not a dangerous woman. To the contrary, she was gentle and helpful. The hospital was seriously underfunded. The cost of maintaining the 280 inmates was limited to 70-cents a day. There were no recreational facilities, so the inmates would wander the corridors aimlessly and at night sleep their anguished sleep. In order to help morale, Winnie Ruth, who had a gift for styling hair, voluntarily shampooed and set the hair of the inmates, using what little money she had to buy shampoo and rinses.

She escaped in 1939, in my second year of high school, and was missing for less than a week. It was the first of her many escapes. However, in 1962, when I had all but ceased thinking about her, she escaped again and made her way to Stockton, California, where she found a job as a companion to the wife of a wealthy physician. Some seven years later, the authorities caught up with her, and returned her to the state hospital.

But just before Christmas, 1971, after 40 years of confinement, she was declared a free woman and she promptly returned to Northern California. In the 1990's she came back to Phoenix to live, using the assumed name of Marion Lane. She passed away in 1998, leaving many unanswered questions about the murders as well as a page crowded with memories in the life of a young man.

16

PHOENIX UNION HIGH still has an active alumni association. It publishes a quarterly newsletter called *The Coyote Journal*, which I read avidly, looking for names I might recognize. Not long ago I saw the name Myrna Handmacher Kaplan in the "In Memoriam" column. She had died at age 81 in Kansas City. According to the death notice, she left two children, both daughters, and several grandchildren. Her husband had predeceased her. Floyd wasn't mentioned. Her death notice was a chilling reminder of how deeply I cared for her, and for Floyd.

It also awakened memories of Katherine. She died in a nursing home in Mesa in her late seventies, a few years before my mother passed away. In the years after my army discharge, I made periodic visits to Phoenix to visit Katherine, at first in her apartment and later on in the nursing home. As always, she greeted me with a bright, welcoming smile. But shortly before she died, she began calling me Floyd. I wasn't put off by that because I had always suspected that, to her, I had become Floyd.

I completely lost track of Rex Alderdice after he and my mother stopped seeing each other. The last time I heard from him was the day before VE Day, May 7, 1945, while I was in Hannover, Germany. It was a postcard written from London and addressed to my APO Box. At that time he had a big job with the office of War Information. I have kept the card all these years.

Dear Arthur:

Have been here about 30 days and hope to complete and return to Paris about June 1. Trust it will be possible to meet you before returning to the States. Should you happen to be in London or Paris during above period please contact me at the OWI office. Your mother writes regularly re her War Bond activities and she is doing a swell job. I hope you are well and trust it won't be too long before you are heading back home.

Kind personal regards and best wishes,
R.A.

Lila and I have been married for well over sixty years. They have not been easy years, mostly because of me. We have seven grandchildren, two of whom live abroad with their parents, the products of our three children.

I don't know a soul in Phoenix today. There are only a few traces left of the city I remember---now so overgrown and heavily trafficked that only the rubble of the past remains.

Several years ago I told Lila about all the things that happened to me in Phoenix---mostly about my strange obsession with Winnie Ruth Judd and my fear of Frank Girvin. As gently as I could, I told her about Myrna and how I was hopelessly in love with her. I didn't leave out a thing. But Lila was disturbed when I told her about Katherine, mainly because she couldn't understand how I could sleep with Katherine at the same time, as she said, that I could have slept with her. I told her about Rabbi Cohen and Dorothy Krakauer and Norm Westerfield and Marvin Hooks. Mostly though I talked about Floyd.

I remember how she fastened her eyes on me as I talked---sympathetic at times, quizzical at others.

When I had finished, she said: "Arthur, are all the things you've told me true? I mean, did they really happen to you?"

I paused for a moment, and then I said: "Of course they did. Kind of."

"What do you mean 'kind of'?" she said.

"Well, they did happen... in a manner of speaking."

--end--

About the Author

M ELVIN MARKS RECENTLY retired as president of a Chicago-based marketing company. He has been a guest lecturer at Northwestern University Graduate School of Management (the Kellogg School) and at John Marshall Law School, Chicago. A newspaperman early in his career, he resumed writing full-time since his retirement.

He is the author of two books of nonfiction: Jews among the Indians and Yesterdays Warriors. His essays have appeared in Chicago Magazine, Across the Board, the New York Times Magazine, Texas, and Western States Jewish History. His work is included in the anthology About Men: Reflections on the Male Experience (Poseidon Press, 1987). Melvin Marks is a veteran of the Second World War and the recipient of four bronze battle stars. He and his wife reside in Chicago.

Printed in the United States
By Bookmasters